TRUE L___ _____ES

SIGNED SEALED AND DELIVERED

OF WOMEN IN POP

D0895806

SUE STEWARD AND SHERYL GARRATT

PLUTO  PRESS

LONDON & SYDNEY

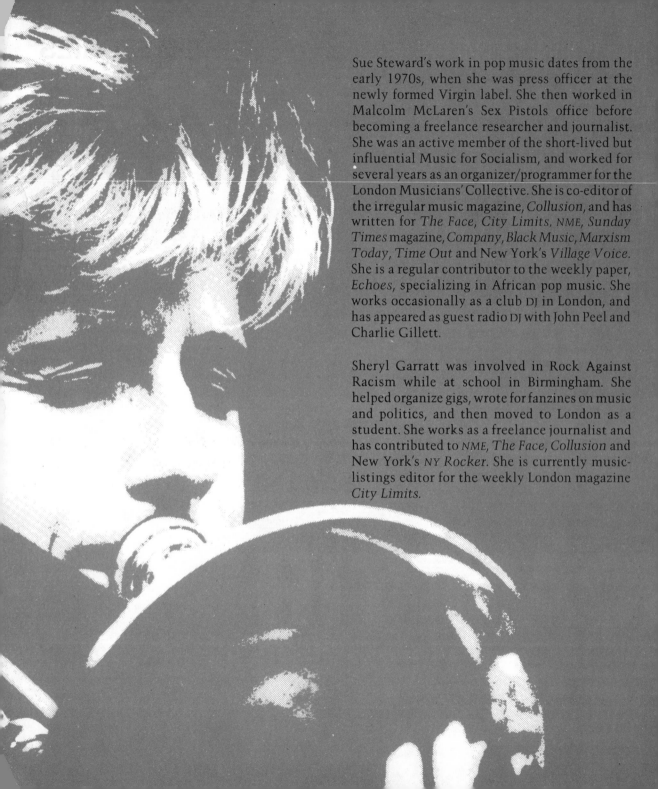

Sue Steward's work in pop music dates from the early 1970s, when she was press officer at the newly formed Virgin label. She then worked in Malcolm McLaren's Sex Pistols office before becoming a freelance researcher and journalist. She was an active member of the short-lived but influential Music for Socialism, and worked for several years as an organizer/programmer for the London Musicians' Collective. She is co-editor of the irregular music magazine, *Collusion*, and has written for *The Face*, *City Limits*, NME, *Sunday Times* magazine, *Company*, *Black Music*, *Marxism Today*, *Time Out* and New York's *Village Voice*. She is a regular contributor to the weekly paper, *Echoes*, specializing in African pop music. She works occasionally as a club DJ in London, and has appeared as guest radio DJ with John Peel and Charlie Gillett.

Sheryl Garratt was involved in Rock Against Racism while at school in Birmingham. She helped organize gigs, wrote for fanzines on music and politics, and then moved to London as a student. She works as a freelance journalist and has contributed to NME, *The Face*, *Collusion* and New York's NY *Rocker*. She is currently music-listings editor for the weekly London magazine *City Limits*.

CONTENTS

First published in 1984 by Pluto Press Limited,
The Works, 105a Torriano Avenue, London NW5 2RX
and Pluto Press Australia Limited,
PO Box 199, Leichhardt, New South Wales 2040, Australia

Copyright © Sue Steward, Sheryl Garratt

Text and cover designed by Caramel at Crunch

Phototypeset by AKM Associates (UK) Ltd.
Ajmal House, Hayes Road, Southall, London
Printed in Great Britain by Photobooks (Bristol) Limited

ISBN 0 86104 657 9

Grace Jones   (photo: David Corio)

ACKNOWLEDGEMENTS

Behind every book is a team. The team behind this one has been endlessly supportive and helpful, and my thanks to them all.

To Sally Townsend for inviting my original article in *Marxism Today* which was the seed for the book, and to Pete Ayrton for persuading Pluto Press that women in pop music are here to stay.

To Sue Scott and Caroline Scott for their contribution to Chapter 9, 'Punkerama'.

To Angela McRobbie for her decisive editorial insight.

To Angela Quinn for her skilful copy editing.

To Simon Frith for his critical support, astute comments, and encouragement always.

To Kate Bradley for her help and her up-to-the-minute musical advice.

To Hannah Charlton for discussion and clarification, and consistent encouragement.

To my flatmates Cherry Smyth and Nick Kimberley for looking after me, body and soul.

To Val Wilmer, for inspiration, stimulation and argument.

To David Toop, for inspiration, encouragement and patience, and for introducing me to a world of new music.

And, finally, to the following women for the time they gave me and for their interviews which made their 'true-life stories' public: Vicki Aspinall; Amazulu; African Woman; Viv Albertine; Abandon Your Tutu; Gina Birch; Belle Stars; Ivy Benson; Janette Beckman; Georgie Born; Kate Bradley; Lindsay Cooper; Carol Colman; Laka Daisical; Ana de Silva; Ann Dudley; Marion Fudger; Frank Chickens (Kazuko Hohki and Kazumi Taguchi); Lotti Golden; Ann Kelly; Barbara Jeffries; Penny Leyton; Carol Kaye; Anne Nightingale; Shirley O'Laughlin; Ruthie Smith; Alison Short; Helen Shapiro; Sandie Shaw; Sheila Tracy; Penny Valentine; Val Wilmer; Annie Whitehead; Carol Wilson; Vicki Wickham.

— Sue Steward

Thanks to all the people who have helped with information, articles and contacts.

Especially, to Julie Burchill for her encouragement; to my editor at *City Limits*, Penny Valentine, whose writing encouraged Caroline Coon; and to Caroline, Vivien Goldman and others who in turn gave me models to follow.

To my flatmates, Noel Halifax and Avril Levi for their patience.

To my parents, Frank and June, for obvious reasons.

To Mark McGuire for his constant help and support.

Thanks, too, to Carrie Booth; Pauline Black; Caroline Coon; Alannah Currie; Hazel O'Connor; Frank Chickens; Vivien Goldman; Jane Hutch; Nazia Hassan; Versa Manos; Robbi Millar; Jona MacDonald; Anne Nightingale; Ranking Ann; Christine Robertson; Sylvia Robinson; Jane Spiers; Vi Subversa; Helen Terry; Ruby Turner; Carroll Thompson; Lesley Woods; Lucy Whitman; Annie Whitehead; and the women at EMI's factory.

— Sheryl Garratt

The Tracy Sisters, Phyl Brown (left) and Sheila Tracy (right), forsook Ivy Benson's All-Girl Dance Band in the '50s, and took their own double trombone act on to the international cabaret circuit. (photo: courtesy of Sheila Tracy)

GHOSTS

IN

THE

HIT MACHINE

SUE STEWARD

'Women in pop music? That'll be a thin book – *are* there any?' a non-music business workmate asked me with incredulity.

'Oh, no, not another book about women in rock,' groaned radio DJ Anne Nightingale in mock horror when I asked her to do an interview for this book. But she agreed all the same.

There are as many contradictions and confusions surrounding the question of women and pop music as there are in any of the fields opened up by feminist analysis. The above two reactions span the gap between the public image of women in pop and the workaday reality. That gap indicates the need for a book revealing exactly how women *do* fit in and fare. The music business is, after all, one of the world's largest leisure industries; despite its size, it's also an industry bent on keeping women out of all but the most traditional roles.

This book is a synthesis of ideas that have been circulating for several years, appearing as articles in a range of magazines. They have been collected together in book form to give a fuller version of the story – primarily as it emerges in Britain, but with plenty of glances round the globe, particularly at the USA.

Like so many other handy labels, 'women in rock' is both intriguing and misleading. It began to circulate in the early 1970s, when there was a closeness between ideals of the women's movement and punk. It was certainly current in 1977 when the TV series *Rock Follies* – a programme about the adventures of a three-woman rock group – began. One way or another, it was around this period that people began to think and talk about the subject of women, sexuality, and pop music. Still, 'women in rock' is a misleading catch-phrase: it reduces women's participation in music to one standard, uniform category – regardless of the differences in their music, outlooks, or ambitions. The same thing happens

with 'black music'. Both labels imply that all women, or all black people in the music industry are doing the same thing.

This tendency was well demonstrated in the book *New Women in Rock* (1981), which packaged together a quirky collection of biographies of women based purely on their gender. Neighbouring pages lump together diverse musicians with no regard for the very different experiences that brought them into music: New York punk poet Patti Smith; Las Vegas cabaret artiste from Nigeria and London Patti Boulaye; the experimental jazz-rock vocalist Annette Peacock; the Scottish middle-of-the-road singer Sheena Easton; and Poly Styrene, the punk screamer from Brixton. *Signed, Sealed and Delivered* takes on this variety and also broadens the musical spectrum to include music ranging from country, jazz, salsa, soul, disco, reggae, African pop, rockabilly, to good old 7" pop. In addition, it looks further into the issues surrounding the women who work within all these different categories.

Our arbitrary starting-point is the mid-1950s, when the *Wild, Wild Young Women (of Rockabilly)* – the title of a Rounder Records round-up of the era – such as Janis Martin, Jean Chapel and Rose Maddox vied for chart positions with Elvis, Gene Vincent and Jerry Lee Lewis. It's a time *before* the male scream heroes had been inflated to fill all available chart- and heart-space with the teeny record-buying public. The UK had no equivalent to pony-tailed 'tom-boys' like Janis Martin or Wanda Jackson, nor was there anybody quite like 'Little' Brenda Lee until the launch of Helen Shapiro in 1960. But the acoustic guitar and rough, tough country singing of those rockabilly women has a lot in common with Chrissie Hynde and a league of American country-rock singers today.

Ruth Brown, 'Miss Rhythm', America's top-selling r 'n b singer throughout the '50s. (photo: courtesy Charlie Gillett)

At that time, too, the tag-enders of the Big Band era – Alma Cogan and Shirley Bassey – were the TV faces of glamour and light entertainment; today the women who occupy such niches – Cilla Black and Lulu – have arrived there after a string of chart successes.

On the fringes of the mainstream chart, but never far from the top of the US soul charts, the legendary 1950s blues and r'n'b singers – LaVern Baker, Ruth Brown ('Miss Rhythm') and Little Esther, among others – laid the foundations for three generations of women soul singers. Their musical descendants are women like Dionne Warwicke, Evelyn 'Champagne' King, Sharon Redd, who occasionally brighten the English mainstream chart landscape; they have also influenced the English–West Indian lovers'-rock style of singing adopted by Jean Adebambo, Janet Kay, Carroll Thompson, and scores of others.

The child-actress-turned-pop-star phenomenon is another link between British women performers today and those from the early postwar years. When Doris Day hit number one with 'Secret Love' and 'Black Hills of Dakota' in 1954, she was already beloved by film-going audiences for her previous roles in musicals such as *Calamity Jane* and *Lullaby of Broadway*, and the cross-over was easy. Petula Clark, a child star who performed for troops during the Second World War, achieved British chart success in 1954 (with 'The Little Shoemaker') and, in the 1960s, became a cult figure in France with her 'Ya Ya Twist'. More recently, London's Italia Conti Theatre School produced child singing-star Lena Zavaroni, and TV comedian Tracey Ullman. The latter has had meteoric success with cover versions including a remake of Doris Day's 'Move over Darling' – and her popularity is as much due to 'period piece' promo videos which use her comedy–mimicry acting as it is to her singing talents.

REWRITING HISTORY

Most books about 'women in rock' tell selective stories; most are glossy fanzines, papier mâché remakes of press-cuttings, press releases, and record company and magazine photographs. Few delve deeper than the conventional questions of the music press to discover how women feel about the way their music is produced, how it feels to be a performer, and their attitudes to their looks, their music, and their fame. Several of the women interviewed said they'd never been asked about being instrumentalists before.

The publishing industry has been alerted to the potential of the music market, realizing that music books can do almost as well as records. However, the glut is mainly in the number of titles, rather than variety or depth of subject-matter, for the same handful of women – Toyah, Debbie Harry, Kate Bush, Siouxsie – reappear time and time again.

The US market is different. Popular music has been a respected academic subject there for many years, and a range of serious books – as well as myriads of fanzine-type paperbacks – reflect that. In many genres, it's possible to glean a fairly balanced picture of women's part. There are, for example, a range of different kinds of writing – biographies, autobiographies, critical analyses and even fiction – on both country and rock music. With jazz, though, even the wealth of books, journals, and magazines were surprisingly male-orientated until Sally Placksin's magnificent *American Women in Jazz* (1982) filled in the other half of the story.

Signed, Sealed and Delivered is, like Sally Placksin's work, an attempt to retrieve women's musical history. It is a gleeful recreation of four decades of popular music. The heroes of rock and roll are recast as ghosts who flit in and out of the stories, useful as keys to time and place, tune and dance, and the normally shadowy women and the handful of well-known faces now occupy

US blues singers were a major inspiration for Alison 'Alf' Moyet, formerly of pop duo Yazoo, now a solo singer.
(photo: Peter Anderson)

the centre-stage. The result is a new version of pop history – built up out of the true-life stories of those women who boosted our own ideas and experiences. Only a tiny percentage of people employed in the record industry live in the public eye or appear in the music press; the majority are backstage in the record companies. As well as talking to the artists themselves, we have gone behind the counter to where the stars – and their acts – are planned, signed, packaged and sold.

We spoke to as many women who were willing to speak to us as we could. By spanning four decades (1950s–1980s), it is possible to identify changes in trends in attitudes towards women working in pop music. Ivy Benson's career as leader of the All-Girls' Dance Band stretches back to the 1940s, when they were considered a 'pop' band. She compares the obstacles facing women who want to get into hard rock and heavy metal bands today with the resistance her 'girls' faced 40 years ago: 'We weren't even accepted into the ballrooms, at first. We were relegated to the tea-shops, and weren't even allowed to join the Musicians' Union. I taught my girls that because it's supposed to be a man's world, they'd have to act on that and match up to the men to get on.' Today, all-women bands can be seen as a gimmicky draw which, initially at least, can be used to their advantage. But, by and large, they will *stay* in the novelty bracket – at the cost of not being taken seriously as performers and musicians. The Belle Stars' waning career sadly illustrates this. There are also bands like Amazulu, who began as all-women reggae performers, but, when casting round for a replacement for their drummer, took 'the most skilled person – who happened to be a man'; they felt they'd passed beyond having to keep the band all-women.

Repeatedly, we were told the same things in our interviews. With great stoical, matter-offactness we heard about the similar obstacles facing women in all areas of the industry, and of the prodigious effort it requires to burst through them. Carol Colman plays bass with Kid Creole and the Coconuts; she is also a trainee studio producer. It was surprising to hear her, a New Yorker, say, 'You have to be twice as smart, twice as tough, and twice as good as the men just to get to the bottom of the rank where you can eat and pay your rent.' That was 1983, New York – a city considered to be far less restrictive for women musicians than Britain is. The most appalling stories were usually told with great relish and bitterness, but mostly 'off the tape'. Some interviewees wouldn't spill the beans about how they were treated at work, or how they viewed their prospects, because that might have jeopardized their future. Some journalists were understandably cagey, realizing only too well how interviews can be twisted and distorted.

Still, this isn't a book of terrible tales (though they would fill one); neither is it a eulogy to glowing *Cosmo*-superwomen who have risen through the male ranks to positions of power, authority, and affluence – those success-stories who also manage to run a home and remain 'nice' people (though there are plenty of those, too). Not surprisingly, we came across a few unambiguously ambitious career women, coated with competitive toughness and a lack of concern for other women's circumstances, forgetful of their own difficult transition.

What this book aims to do is to challenge the partial picture presented in newspaper, magazine, book, TV and radio reports. Anything selling outside of the chart recording shops remains outside the mainstream catchment – and few people would guess that some soca, reggae, lovers'-rock and, particularly, soul and dance music sometimes outsell 'chart' records. The general public's conception of pop is based on a weekly viewing of *Top of the Pops* or the pop magazine-shows, and occasional listening to the radio.

It isn't that these music books and magazines and TV and radio programmes actually peddle lies or even blatantly distort. They simply leave the women out. So, just as we are trying to rewrite the history of pop, we are simultaneously challenging what is pumped out as definitive in the standard 'History of . . .' type of radio series.

Part of the problem of rewriting the story from a feminist angle is that women have often been made quite invisible. Of course, they are taken for granted as frontline singers. Even then, though, they can have a double-edged status: audience focus, leader, but also 'just the singer', not skilled like the instrumental backline. That isn't so true in soul or country music where the voice is prized like an instrument.

There's no doubt that punk marked a turning-point as far as this was concerned. It must be said that punk euphoria carried women as well as men along on its tide, but that shouldn't blind us to the way the industry swiftly managed to curtail the invasion of the 'wild women of punk' in the time-honoured methods reserved for women in pop. It trivialized them, glamorized them and neutralized them . . . But it didn't silence them. In some ways, it was punk's noisiness which helped make this book happen.

In the wake of punk, there have been positive developments in women's music – more so in the USA than in Britain. The new genre 'women's music' has grown out of labels like Olivia and Redwood, produced by and for women, and distributed through a grassroots network. While their music isn't exactly new in form (being inspired mainly by folk and jazz), the methods of organizing and producing it set it apart from the rest of the industry – and prove that it *is* possible to operate outside the conventional multi-national structure to quite a degree. In Britain, the original women's movement mascot band of the mid-1970s, Jam Today, eventually established their own Stroppy Cow label, and released their own single, 'Stereotyping'. Large-scale initiatives like Oliva and Redwood are lacking in Britain – a situation that might be rectified by the recent formation of Birmingham Women's Revolutions Per Minute, who are now building a network to supply shops.

As we drew to a close with *Signed, Sealed and Delivered* we were frustratingly aware of how much we had to leave out, how many interviews we didn't do and also how rapidly the female faces in pop change. Each chapter could be (and hopefully will be) expanded into a whole book.

There *is* something artificial about binding together women in this way – obviously every kind of music has its own rules, conditions and standards, its own aesthetic and economic relationships. Nevertheless, there *are* some unchanging underlying factors, shared and experienced by all women venturing into the international pop music industry – from Annie Mae Bullock (Tina Turner) to Annie Lennox, the Dixie Cups to the Belle Stars. It has been exciting to discover new women working in areas we previously thought were male domains: Ann Dudley, a commercial pop record producer; Corinne Simcock, a studio engineer; Carroll Thompson, singer–songwriter, producer and record company co-director; and Carol Wilson, who single-handedly runs an independent record label. All are still rare species in Britain, but in the USA such roles are no longer exclusive to men.

Altogether, I tend towards realistic optimism about the future of women in pop music. One week's *Top of the Pops* can be a journey back into the dark ages. The only women in sight are either gooey schoolgirls aimlessly waving banners for the cameras, or the contortionists dressed in some version of fetish-wear, who dance self-consciously to four-square rhythms pumped out by white macho-boys. But then along comes a group like the Fun Boy Three, where the three pretty funboys were out front singing 'Our Lips are Sealed', while the 'business' – the music – was carried on by a seven-piece band of women, who played everything from cello to trombone behind them. On such occasions we know there's no going back. Women are not condemned to be passive, swooning onlookers while the boys have all the fun on stage.

Fun Boy Three during its 1983 chart-topping phase.
(photo: Brian Cooke/Chrysalis Records)

13

CHAPTER ONE

AGENTS

O ★ ★ ★ ★ F

STYLE

SUE STEWARD & SHERYL GARRATT

Sadé Adu's background as a fashion designer and her assured sense of classic style were as much responsible for her entry into the 1980s pop scene as her vocal qualities.   (photo: Joe Bangay, courtesy Epic Records)

JUST ONE LOOK

Think of all the songs that make it clear from the start that it is image and impression, style and presentation, that count. It's not surprising that many of these songs have been written and performed by men; inevitably they've been bowled over by 'just one look' or by the way that, though she was 'just 17' (you know what I mean?), the way she looked was way beyond compare . . . It is looks and appearance, but most of all style, which have prompted ecstatic song, music, rhythm and dance.

In music, an image can develop slowly and organically, changing as the performer changes, or it can be a rushed creation dictated by the demands of the media. The possibility of a sudden hit record can mean a supervised visit to the hairdressers and a make-up artist, a new set of clothes and a photo-session where the new look that will help sell the product is put together. The process is the same for men and women, only men can get away with less adornment. One of the familiar stereotypes of women performers is the idea of a production-line of looks: a star groomed and dressed like a Barbie Doll, passed from expert to expert. Sheena Easton is often discussed in this way; and the TV documentary on her early rise to fame, *The Big Time*, reinforced the idea. What the programme did *not* show was how Sheena had fought to be featured on it in the first place, her single-minded determination to be a star at all costs. Though at first, perhaps, she appeared to be a puppet, it has since become clear how thoroughly she understands the workings of the music machine – the need not only to produce records, but to perform well for the media, and, most of all, to look 'right'.

Inevitably, the definition of the word 'right' changes all the time, and although the rules are mostly unwritten, most of us know what is or isn't fashionable – and dress either to blend or to be noticed. We follow the rules or choose to break them, and when every sartorial detail is loaded and coded, it is impossible to be spontaneous. Some may dismiss any interest in trends, claiming to dress only for themselves; this, however, is never totally persuasive. Our thefts from the past are selective, and even the rebels have their limits and restrictions.

There's no such thing as 'natural'. Despite the illusion of anarchy and endless variety which has built up since the 1970s, image is always governed by the social and political climate and by fashion, by the record companies and by the media, by the demands – and even hazards – of a live audience. The age, race and culture of the individual involved, as well as the conventions of the type of music she is performing also exert their influence. This is true whether she sings film soundtracks in Bombay, country ballads in Nashville, or post-punk love songs in Glasgow. Each genre of music has its own conventions. Imagine Beki Bondage wearing a long, formal evening gown to sing at the Marquee Club. Or Loretta Lynn appearing at the Grand Ole Opry in a leather jacket and ripped fishnet tights.

Some women choose to abide by, and so maintain, these rules; others relish breaking or subverting them to create precedents for change. Dolly Parton in her wig and rhinestones is a parody of the ultra-feminine country woman; Patti Smith, in her tough boots and misshapen men's suit-jackets, was still unmistakably female – but not at all 'feminine' – and challenged the ideas of what women rock performers should look like. The images of both women were at least partly responsible for their successes.

Other women, however, are not so lucky – and pay dearly for breaking the rules. Hazel O'Connor was scorned by the press when she appeared on *Top of the Pops* in a mini-skirt and bikini top, showing a white body and a midriff a little flabbier than the fashion magazines deem appro-

The blonde-haired, wind-blown look of Tammy Wynette, the idol of millions of female country music fans.
(photo: Norman Seeff, courtesy Epic Records)

priate. Others have disappeared into oblivion because they refused to conform. Even for success-ful women, the constant need to justify them-selves in public, or to ignore the attacks made on them, can lead to drink, drugs, depression. Janis Joplin is, of course, the classic tragedy. Others lose their individuality, or are destroyed by their concern to fit in at all costs. Karen Carpenter's obsession with her weight eventually cost her her life, as a victim of anorexia.

Though the effects are not so extreme for most, it is still important to recognize that choices *are* controlled and limited – and far more for women than for men. Female roles and stereotypes are far more restrictive, the standards of perfection so much higher, and the pressures on women to conform with their bodies, their faces and their clothes, much greater.

THE NAME GAME

In the music industry names, like clothing, are often clues to the type of music the artist performs. In retrospect, they often place their bearers chronologically, too. Names can be changed to convey the desired impression: Annie Mae Bullock became sex goddess Tina Turner; plain and frumpy Priscilla White became snappy 1960s girl, Cilla Black. Country singer Kitty Wells took her name from the old English folksong 'Sweet Kitty Wells' (which perfectly evokes the old-fashioned Ole Opry era), whereas Crystal Gayle (Brenda Webb) is a name with a more recent, though no less country, ring. Sister

Nancy and Ranking Ann could only be reggae sistren, while Poly Styrene, Cherry Vanilla, or Gaye Advert obviously grew up, musically, in the mid-1970s.

Prefixes like 'Little' and 'Big' distinguish one Richard or Walter, Eva or Esther, from another. They also reveal the likely race of the artists and their kind of music. When 'Little' stars grow up, they are faced with either dropping the tag – as 'Little' Stevie Wonder did – or taking a new name to match their adult status. 'Little' Esther – hit-making singer with the Johnny Otis Band in the 1950s – took her new name, Phillips, from an oil-company advertising hoarding. 'Little' Eva, her 'Locomotion' days over, kept the tag and its associations into adulthood, but never repeated her youthful success.

Male jazz musicians traditionally dubbed themselves with lofty titles: 'Count', 'Duke', 'Earl', 'King'. The same honorifics are used by some of today's African pop stars (Nigeria's King Sunny Ade, and Queen Salawa Abeni). With a few exceptions – Billie 'Lady Day' Holiday; 'The Empress' Bessie Smith; or 'The Duchess', Bo Diddley's guitar partner – women have tended to rely on titles which describe their size or status as women: 'Big' (Maybelle), 'Little' (Esther), 'Mama' (Yancey), Ma (Rainey).

In the 1960s, London impresario Larry Parnes launched a nest of shy young men on to the English pop scene, countering their ordinariness first of all with new names. His protégés achieved fame under names that were positive, aggressively male, or just plain catchy: Power, Eager, Gentle, Fury, Pride and Wilde. There was Reg Smith – 'a big tall lad of 6'4" '. He had to be made friendly, so 'Reg' became 'Marty'; he also had to be sneeringly tough, so 'Smith' went 'Wilde'.

A name's importance in contributing to image is well recognized. Choosing a name for a group can be a headache – often providing good copy later. One of the first all-women rock bands was the US quartet Fanny, whose name is a calculated mixture of female associations. In the 1980s, Fanny could be an all-male, heavy metal band; in the early 1970s, there was no mistaking the gender of the group who were the original 'women in rock'. The name was tough, slightly ironic, slightly self-derisory – features it shares with the punk names of a few years later. The latter, though, were more blatant and unambiguous: the Bloods, PMT, Snatch, IUDs, Penetration, the Castrators. While Fanny doesn't have totally positive associations for women, it is more sanitized than the name which led the uprising of punk women – the Slits. The band's former guitarist, Viv Albertine, still relishes the pleasure they got from their name: 'Taxidrivers, our mothers, feminists, men – no one liked it. It was obscene to everybody. But the DJs didn't like it, either – so it did have adverse effects. If we had stayed together, we would have changed the name.' Viv thinks the name existed before she joined the group, coined by the then-bassist, American Kate Korus: 'In America, it's slang for a woman – not a particularly complimentary one, but Palmolive [drummer] and Ari [singer] being Spanish and German, had no idea of the word's connotations for a long time. For them it was just a very short, sharp word, which sounded clean and easy to remember – an ideal punk name.'

A name can be a hindrance, too. It's difficult to swap once a band has a following, unless the swap is used to mark a musical or conceptual change of identity. That is what happened in 1980 when the all-women Body Snatchers mutated into the Belle Stars. The name-change coincided with the replacement of two of the more radical feminist members. The Body Snatchers dropped their more self-conscious political stance in favour of a more traditional, commercial, glam-girls-in-rock identity – the Belle Stars.

Group names are subject to vogues like anything else in pop. Eras tend to be identifiable by group names as much as fashion styles. The typical all-women group in the 1960s was a trio or quartet of harmony-singing black (or imitative white) women, whose collective identity had to end in -elle or, preferably, -ette. This was the heyday of the Shirelles, the Bluebelles, the Marvelettes, and the group that perhaps epitomizes the era, the Ronettes. The dictionary

Neat trouser suits, black wigs and sweet expressions belie the furore whipped up by the Ronettes in the '60s, when girls were still supposed to look like Helen Shapiro. (photo: courtesy Charlie Gillett)

19

defines -ette as indicating smallness, imitation or substitute, or the female version ... Since the 1960s, -ette has been used particularly for female back-up trios: Ray Charles's Raelettes; Ike and Tina's Ikettes; and the more recent tongue-in-cheek grossness of Bette Midler's Harlettes; and the reverent nostalgia of the Eurythmics' Croquettes. Even Adam Ant's first group had back-up singers called, in suitable punk mode, the Lillettes.

CARAPACES AND WHALEBONES
The early 1950s was the era of fan-tailed carapaces encrusted with sequins, and glamorous dresses which filled the monochrome TV screens of the nation's dining-rooms. The women inside them were the 'belters', whose powerful voices wreaked havoc with our parents' emotions, and whose dresses were the talking-point of the day. Tailing off from the Big Band era of the previous decade were singers like Ann Shelton and Ruby Murray and all-women dance bands such as Ivy Benson's, whose costumes had to be slightly more practical, but no less formal.

Slinky, sensuous, Eartha Kitt and Shirely Bassey created sensations in backless, full-length dresses. Shirley Bassey's were often fitted so tight she had to be lifted on stage. These were sophisticated, sexy images for women who, in the austere aftermath of the war, yearned for 'an old-fashioned millionaire', or, later, 'a big spender'. Then there was Alma Cogan in her rigid *Come Dancing* frocks. The daughter of a tailor, Alma Cogan was always introduced as the woman who had hand-sewn all her own creations. Restricted in their fantastic armour, these women were literally held together by whalebones and zips.

With the arrival of rock'n'roll, the boys discarded their tuxedos and kept on their street clothes to sing, but Alma and the girls were still dressed for a ball ... In white shirts, dark ties and suits, Cliff Richard and Adam Faith looked just

like other boys of their own age. But the only women who dressed like their fans were the folksinging chanteuses – Judith Durham (the Seekers) and Dusty Springfield (the Springfields), the US rockabilly women (Janis Martin, Wanda Jackson, etc.), and the country singers who, like Patsy Cline, went for gingham dresses with frills or pedal-pushers and pony-tails. The nearest equivalent in the UK to those rocking women were a few skifflers in the Nancy Whiskey and Beryl Bryden mould. But several of the Americans spent extended periods in the British charts: Wanda Jackson had 70 hits here around the end of the 1950s. In 1960, 14-year-old Brenda Lee first arrived in Britain with 'Sweet Nothings', marking the dawn of a new era of pop music. Helen Shapiro, also 14, was launched in 1961, as 'The British Brenda Lee'. Though mermaid dresses had given way to shorter, 'ballerina' lengths, and less formal styles, the gap between the wardrobes of these girl stars and those of their fans remained as wide as ever.

Interviewed 22 years after her peak of success, Helen still vividly remembers how much she loathed those costumes (lady dresses, court shoes and gloves) and the gulf between her and the fans:

> When I sang 'Don't Treat Me Like A Child', it was from the heart. I was 14, being managed and groomed as a child star, with little say in the matter. They used to tell me not to wear jeans, to stay in my dressing-room and not talk to the others on the show [which later included the Beatles]. But I never took any notice of what they said – except for the stage dresses, where I had to bow to other people's superior knowledge.

Alma Cogan (left) is unfairly remembered more for her dress designs than her voice, whilst Connie Francis (right) never had to live down such a memory. Skiffle King Lonnie Donnegan, models his teeth. (photo: courtesy Charlie Gillett)

21

They were awful! I dropped them as soon as I could, and got into something a little more realistic. Those great thousand yards of tulle were beautifully made, but I was never comfortable in all those bones and tight waists. What I wanted to do, like all the girls of my age, was to wear my spikey shoes, pencil skirt, and baggy sweater.

There are publicity photographs which show that occasionally she got her way. Nevertheless, the image of Helen Shapiro which lasts to this day is of a lacquered Cindy Doll, with a beehive helmet, high heels and a short ballgown.

While Helen was 'Walking Back to Happiness' in 1961, she shared the charts with the Shirelles, whose number one hit, 'Will You Love Me Tomorrow?', marked the dawn of the classic 'girl group' era, and the birth of new looks. By 1963, Dusty Springfield had gone solo, influenced in both her looks and in her music by black American singers and girl groups. Her appearance became increasingly stylized, with sculpted wigs and bejewelled cocktail dresses.

The 'sweetness and passivity' myth of the early girl groups (photographed clumped together with identical clothes and smiles) evolved into an altogether tougher, street-wise identity. Groups like the Ronettes and Shangri-Las typified the new image. Sparks would often fly between the Shangri-Las and their songwriter, Ellie Greenwich, who remembers tears in the toilets, shouting matches, and criticisms about the girls' looks (ripped stockings!), behaviour (gum-chewing and lateness), and bad language – parent–child conflicts for a top-selling, trendsetting group.

'Don't treat me like a child': Helen Shapiro, a schoolgirl by day, and reluctantly encased in stiff dresses by night. Today, Helen is comfortable in her own choice of both songs and costumes.
top: courtesy of Helen Shapiro   left: courtesy EMI records
bottom: Oval Records

FROM TULLE TO ASTRO-GARB
Most young women in this country saw the US acts (Supremes, Ronettes, Lesley Gore, Aretha Franklin, Dionne Warwicke) alongside the home products (Lulu, Cilla Black, Sandie Shaw, Dusty

Springfield, Marianne Faithfull) on the weekly pop TV show, *Ready Steady Go!* (RSG) and on package tours. These women, along with Mary Quant, transformed the wardrobes of British girls. Satin and tulle were discarded in favour of the new style – shockingly casual, definitely not dressed-up in the accepted meaning of the words. 'You can't go out dressed like that, you're not "dressed-up",' became the favourite parental reproach. On stage and TV, our heroines had rising-by-the-week beehives, short, straight 'shift' dresses, or – the biggest shock for parents – trouser suits. The style was casual and semi-sporty.

Looking back at the videos of RSG, it is surprising how prophetic they seem. Lulu *bounced*, exuded great confidence and joy at dancing on the little stage in her matelot top and tight hipster pants. Cilla Black always wore dresses, quite demure, often with ruffles at the neck and cutaway sleeves to exaggerate her bony shoulders. She looked gawky and angular and quite ordinary, but her confidence as a singer – as she unselfconsciously wove through her fans, looking straight to camera – revealed her as a natural entertainer. Lulu and Cilla were clearly destined to move on from singing into the broader pastures of 'variety'. Sandie Shaw, by

LaBelle's manager, Vicki Wickham, (centre) seen here backstage with Patti LaBelle (left) and Sarah Dash (right) before they climbed into their fantastic armoured costumes to lead the glam rock movement. (photo: Val Wilmer/Format)

contrast, never looked very comfortable as a performer: shy and awkward, almost frowning as she walked and sang (maybe because she was very short-sighted and, like John Lennon, not allowed to wear her specs). But she was marvellous as a model – the face of the era – and better on record than live.

Unlike these clearly ordinary girls who'd had a lucky break, Dusty Springfield already had a career behind her when her solo songs hit the charts. She was never girlish; her costumes were formal; her songs, like Sandie's and Cilla's, were mostly cover versions of US hits, which she interpreted with the complicated, jerky, sign-language gestures copied from the Motown groups. While Sandie performed with her hands by her side, Lulu bounced and jived, and Cilla – wringing the meaning of songs with her thrusting hands – was reminiscent of Shirley Bassey.

The 'narrative' groups, like the Shangri-Las, relied more on group involvement, meaningful looks, mock shock, to tell their mini-epics. They never went through the tulle frocks phase: their earlier photographs reveal four (one was ditched early on) very preppy, WASP girls, with neat flick-ups or plaited hair 'put up', and decidedly secretarial outfits, tweedy skirts and polo tops. A far cry from their later US beatnik look, which so scared the parents of 1960s teenage girls: black leather waistcoats, white shirts, straight pants, and leather boots.

Vicki Wickham, a producer and programmer for RSG, recollects another New York girl group, Patti LaBelle and the BlueBelles, coming to the show. She remembers their transition from tulle to astro-garb.

> The routines, the doowop, and the pretty dresses had all gone out of vogue by then. Luckily, when the girls came to RSG they'd all been to Biba's that day, and looked so good in their new clothes that we said, "Don't change, *please!*" Otherwise it would

Nona Hendryx's changing musical directions have always matched her shifting visual identity, continuing Labelle's policy of rejecting the market's restricting styles for black singers.
(photo: courtesy RCA Records)

have been back to the "taffeta dresses" – awful! And they didn't.

Instead, Barbara Hulanicki's (owner and designer of Biba) geometric patterns, padded shoulders, and futuristic versions of Hollywood 1940s costumes paved the way for the group's spectacular metamorphosis into the pioneering group of glam-rock, LaBelle. LaBelle's marketing concepts set them apart from many other groups attempting to shrug off early 1960s images. Vicki Wickham left London for New York, to help the transformation:

> My concept for them was 'Don't treat them like a black girl group, treat them like you would the Stones or the Who.' And the only thing we could think of to attract attention was the costumes. We had to have something dramatic otherwise people would have thought it was Patti LaBelle and the BlueBelles again. There was a New York designer, Larry LeGaspi, who wanted to get outrageous, so we said 'Go for it!' And that was where it all came from. In fact, Kiss used Larry for their costumes years later.

After 1967, the girl group era really waned. In the USA, the pop face of black pride – where nationalist politics intersected with commercialism – meant discarding straight wigs and processed hair-dos. LaBelle burnt their wigs, went 'natural' and had a minor hit with Gil Scott-Heron's song, 'The Revolution Will Not Be Televised'. But the early part of the decade had established a new correspondence between street and stage looks.

As the 1960s progressed, street fashion was led from the stage. The lucrative marriage between the ragtrade and the pop industry was celebrated on RSG, in the pages of the glossy magazines, and on the catwalks of the fashion houses. Models' lives became closely entwined with this new social whirl of photographers, pop stars and journalists. Together they created the myths of the 'Swinging 60s' in 'Swinging London'.

Sandie Shaw arrived in the public eye in 1967, wearing A-line dresses made and designed by her or her friends. The economic relationship between pop and the ragtrade is taken for granted today: Vivienne Westwood commercialized the looks of punk, and subsequently focused the New Romantics through the pirate costumes she made for Annabella LuWin of BowWowWow. But the bond that seems to have been there for ever was, in fact, new when Sandie Shaw's career started. Her straight, slinky hair was the new style: hair conditioner advertisements replaced those for lacquer. Sandie, with RSG presenter Cathy McGowan and, eventually, Lulu, all designed clothes and put their names to fashion lines (which Lulu still does, through the Freeman's catalogues, while Cathy went on to run a classy second-hand clothes boutique). Sandie's first husband, designer Jeff Banks, provided her fans with cheap, stylish separates. Sandie, by now darling of the fashion pages, acted as a model. Her choice to continue to look like the girls in the audience after she became a top pop star refreshed the industry, and gave her a fast-rising career as a model as well as a singer:

> I was introduced to Deirdre McSharry, who was fashion editor of the Daily Express, and I told her how I designed my own clothes. She said, 'Design me some and I'll get them made up for you – you can model them as well, if you like.' So I did. I modelled them for the Daily Express, and then Queen, which was the mag of the time, discovered me and put me on the cover.

European countries have their own pop histories, of course. In the early 1960s, a few French singers, particularly Françoise Hardy, had some chart – and fashion – success in Britain. With her long, straight, brown hair, black eyeliner, droopy sweaters and straight pants, Françoise represented the updated commercial face of 1950s existentialist café society, epitomized by Juliette Greco. Her style was also a likely inspiration for an impressionable English schoolgirl aware of her own European ancestry, Marianne Faithfull, and for the German singer Nico, who took her classic melancholic beauty to New York's Velvet Underground. Françoise Hardy was never more than a fleeting novelty act, but her later modelling (particularly of Courrège's white leather ankle-boots) left their mark on the English fashion scene for some time.

BAUBLES, BANGLES ... AND BEADS

By the end of the 1960s, one designer – Barbara Hulanicki – and her Aladdin's cave emporium, Biba – was the major, single influence on the looks of a whole generation of young women. Through Biba's mail-order service, even those outside London could look like the models they envied in the glossy mags, and the movies about Swinging London. Reasonably priced, but outrageously fashionable outfits arrived at your door in tasteful black cardboard boxes, crammed with tissue-paper, to make you the envy of the party.

Biba gave us a look for working, for playing (and, later, for domestic decor too) and it also revolutionized certain items of clothing on a mass scale. It popularized the T-shirt (imagine life before T-shirts!), inaugurated the cult of cheap, gaudy accessories (baubles, boas, badges, and beads). Barbara Hulanicki's designs owed a lot to the 1930s and 1940s: padded shoulders, bold patterns, folds, drapes, gathers, and plenty of glitz for evenings. Never far away was the soft 'feminine' look – conjuring up the image of a romantic heroine in an Arthur Rackham painting, or a prewar Hollywood movie. Though the underlying emphasis was certainly on 'femininity', new definitions were emerging to stretch the traditional associations of vulnerability/ passivity (which Biba offered as well, via the soft-focus images of Sarah Moon's advertising photographs). Fashion encompassed ghoulish, vampiric looks which predated Siouxsie-punk;

black and maroon colours darkened lips; and panda-eyes were made-up with bottle, plum and navy eye-shadow.

By then, women in pop music were braving the harsh climate of an industry which expected them to conform to a very limited number of stereotypes. The options for women were both polarized and few, ranging between two extremes: virgin or whore. Both extremes were perpetuated by the media's reactions and their pigeon-holing of any woman venturing on stage. However, it was these women who laid the foundations for the more obvious presence of a few years later.

The diversity of images thrown up by the 1960s and early 1970s inspired *Melody Maker's* 1972 conference about 'Women in Rock'. An assortment of women performers were invited to debate the issues – particularly the new awareness around looks, and women's sexuality. Both subjects were being publicly discussed for the first time, especially by Marion Fudger in the pages of the recently founded feminist magazine, *Spare Rib*. Marion Fudger, bass-player with the Derelicts, reported the conference in her column in *Spare Rib*, paying special attention to those polarized images that had dominated the 1960s: rock whore and folksong virgin.

Elkie Brooks, then singing with Vinegar Joe, admitted that she had actually been singing 'for ever' but that 'until I started putting myself across sexually, wearing slits up the side and little bikini tops, nobody wanted to know. In some ways I feel bad about the option.'

Mary Hopkin, the Welsh folksinger, had appeared on *Opportunity Knocks* and was a Paul McCartney venture. She was described as 'the epitome of the passive feminine role', 'England's sweetheart – a naive country hick'. Marion Fudger explained how such stereotyped vulnerability and passivity could reduce the chances of a woman being taken seriously as an artist.

Elkie's slashed skirts and Mary's virginal

The year 1973. *Melody Maker* organized a discussion on women, music, and sexuality, with (from left to right) Elkie Brooks (then with Vinegar Joe), Marion Fudger (*Spare Rib*), Maddy Prior (Steeleye Span), Yvonne Elliman (vocalist for top blues-rock bands), Marsha Hunt (solo singer), and hosted by Rob Partridge (*Melody Maker*).   (photo: courtesy Marion Fudger)

choirgirl dresses and flowing blonde hair represent the extremes of the limited guises open to white performers of the time: singing in front of an all-male band, or solo as a folksy singer-songwriter with acoustic guitar. As always, black women of the time – Linda Lewis, Marsha Hunt, P.P. Arnold – fitted uneasily into both niches.

Speaking on the *Melody Maker* panel, Marsha Hunt compared the options open to women generally with those available to black performers trying to wedge themselves into the industry: 'You've got to slip in through the side-door as the statutory representative – and once you're in, then you do your damage, but you're kidding yourself if you think you're going to get in on your own terms.'

Some months previously, Marsha had advertised her new single, 'Oh, No, Not The Beast

Day', in *Spare Rib*. She'd worn a white three-piece man's suit, silk tie, dark glasses, cropped hair and had a cigarette hanging from her lips. Behind her, the band (all men) lounged in identical outfits. Marsha Hunt didn't look like a woman slipping through any side-doors – she was tackling, head on, the options open to women, especially to black women. Her Afro-halo was now shorn to a Nina Simone-style 'natural' crop, which in the USA was a symbol of black consciousness. Her cross-dressing separated her sharply from images purveyed by other women in the contemporary charts: Olivia Newton-John's nauseating goody-goodyness, Nancy Sinatra's hard professionalism, Carly Simon's liberated raunch, or even Suzi Quatro's leather tantrums. Marsha Hunt was a confident parody of tough-guy ease, of a stereotype that wasn't even 'officially' open to her as a black singer.

Throughout the 1970s, women like Marsha Hunt and, later, Patti Smith continued to challenge traditional stereotypes. And people continued to talk about the meanings of female images. Patti Smith, particularly, encouraged awareness of the connection between how we look and how we view ourselves, and was an important influence on the events of 1976, when the few women going into rock bands mostly clung to the traditional 'feminine' looks. They still exposed or exaggerated the erogenous zones with slashed skirts, cutaway tops, diaphanous dresses. Though frequently claimed to express a newly found sexual liberation and freedom from hang-ups about the body, these clothes told the same old story – but with new contradictions.

The two most significant women in rock music at the time, Grace Slick (of Jefferson Airplane) and Janis Joplin (of Big Brother and the Holding Company and, later, Full Tilt), both worked out of the West Coast of the USA. Their influence was felt in Britain, partly in their different but equally strong vocal styles, and partly in their dress-sense. Janis and Grace both revelled in an image of heavy drinking, drug-taking and loving, though Janis couldn't cope and eventually died through it. The enduring picture of her is of an angry, confused woman, swigging Southern Comfort between lines of her blues re-recreations, shrieking and raging. Her songs became anthems for a generation of frustrated women. Grace Slick, the Queen of Rock, seemed to have things more sorted out. She was a powerful woman who brought up her child and still managed to boast of 'tripping' once a week. Both wore clothes which today carry all kinds of negative associations for women.

Janis built an identity for an era out of her own shifting, bag-lady wardrobe, layering together jewellery, feather boas and beads, waistcoats, loose tops, and prints that clashed with embroi-

deries. It was a style that formed the basis of what has become known as the 'hippy look' for women on both sides of the Atlantic. Today, that look has lost many of its positive associations, becoming synonymous with passive Earth-mother types who are generally put upon by their men (and children), and who drift around in aimless dependence and vulnerability. However, in the 1970s that look was taken as the expression of a woman who *did* enjoy her sexuality. American women of rock – especially Grace Slick and Carly Simon – celebrated feeling sexual, were easy about the 'image' they put over, and were as happy to be photographed in slinky clothes, as with their babies and children.

A new awareness of ecology and neo-ruralism (back to the land) and Eastern philosophies also added to the composite hippy identity, and each element carried its own sartorial details.

A number of English women also fell for the blues via Janis. Maggie Bell (then with Stone the Crows), and Christine Perfect (with Chicken Shack, and later, as McVie, with Fleetwood Mac) adopted the same kinds of mixed dress, embodying the same contradictions.

A particularly English genre, folk-rock, involved many women too. In sweet, pure, choirgirl voices, these singers developed a style which can still be seen, fossilized, at folk festivals today. But they weren't simpering, pretty things either – their whole lifestyle was just as much 'one of the boys' as was the Blues women's. Perhaps they got less respect for it because their songs were resurrections of English folksongs, and generally romantic themes of bygone times, rather than the political rallying cries of their American counterparts. The folk-rock movement in the USA, under the leadership of Joan Baez, Judy Collins, and Joni Mitchell (all identikits of acoustic guitar, long straight hair and peasant skirts) roused a generation of white anti-war students into action. Buffy St Marie adopted her native American Indian costumes to sing about *their* plight, while Melanie tagged behind, cooing sweet, ineffectual, lukewarm protests which followed her for years.

The hippy era also witnessed a flirtation with androgyny, although this took a different form from the Annie Lennox version of today and the exploration of sexuality through experiments with images was very much a male prerogative (Country Joe McDonald, David Bowie, among others). However, as the 1970s progressed women were drawn to androgyny (or 'unisex', as it was known): Suzi Quatro's pallid leather 'tomboy' was, admittedly, not an image that asked any questions about sexuality; Patti Smith's outsize men's jackets and conspicuous trilbies *did*.

SAFETY-PINS AND STILETTOES

... Then there was punk. It's always surprising, looking back at the photos taken at the time, how tame it all seems now. The clothes favoured by many of the earlier fans – mohair sweaters, straight trousers, baggy shirts worn with ties, leather jackets – were on sale in Chelsea Girl chain stores within a couple of years (minus the pins and slogans, of course) ... Designer Zandra Rhodes, however, got in on the act at the start, when she turned the safety-pin into a costly diamante accessory before it had barely become a nationwide punk essential. Some of the pictures of Siouxsie Sioux in 1976 look remarkably similar to Sheena Easton at the time of her *Modern Girl* debut four years later. But in spite of the commercial ragtrade's rapid cashing-in and the speed at which mainstream pop adopted the looks of punk, there *was* a revolution of sorts. Suddenly, women stopped dressing to be exclusively attractive to men and chose instead looks that were more or less deliberately repulsive (except for Siouxsie, who from the start was the perversely glamorous go-go girl).

Bedroom fantasy-clothes were worn in the street, thanks to Vivienne Westwood's and Malcolm McLaren's Sex boutique. But the usual meanings of leather, rubber, bondage, suspender-belts, fishnet tights, short skirts and see-through tops were reversed by the way in which they were worn: aggressively confrontational and defiantly asexual. 'People keep away from me. They sort of stand away and look on. They think I'm very cold,' said Jordan, one of the early punk figures, in *Spare Rib*. 'The press have given the impression that I'm a hard bitch. I'm not vampy or an ogre, but I've been to places where they've had bets on who's got the nerve to dance with me.'

Femininity was either hidden, or parodied and made grotesque. Make-up became, literally, a mask; for a while performers were free to choose their own images, to invent a persona to hide behind. For Siouxsie, it was Ice Queen/Dominatrix – a cold, sharp-tongued exterior behind which she kept the audience at bay and jealously guarded her private life from prying journalists. Sometimes shown in photographs looking soft and vulnerable, she could quickly become rigid and cold again, an image that also suited her wailing Teutonic voice. Faye Fife of the Rezillos customized 1960s kitsch inventing a whacky, unreal, cartoon stage-character, while Poly Styrene used Day-Glo and crimplene suits to emphasize her songs.

Poly Styrene remains the sharpest commentator on looks, self-image and society. With a white mother and a black father, she was born an outsider, having to create her own racial identity just as she later created identities for others, selling clothes in the King's Road market. When Poly crashed on stage, arms flailing, hair wild and frizzy, and that tooth-brace glinting, some hailed her as a revolutionary, a woman performing at last as herself. But Poly, singing 'Art-I-Ficial', knew that nature had nothing to do with it:

*I know I'm artificial
But don't put the blame on me
I was reared with appliances
In a consumer society
When I put on my make-up
The pretty little mask not me
That's the way a girl should be
In a consumer society.*

Poly eventually began to see spaceships, retired quietly, and found a *new* identity as a mother and in Hare Krishna.

The Slits changed from leather and jeans à la Runaways and Gaye Advert (the rock'n'roll uniform) to skirts, ribbons, warpaint and, eventually, a dubious hotchpotch of tribalism and Rasta imagery. America sanitized punk somewhat. Wendy 'O' Williams and her band, the Plasmatics, attempted to turn live gigs into sex shows – shocking, maybe, but, unlike the glorious unselfconsciousness of the Slits, never subversive. In spite of Wendy's claims about liberation and the celebration of the female body, her shows serve only to reinforce the old ideas about women as ornaments. Debbie Harry played similar double-edged games. She is a brilliant bubblegum compilation of American fantasy, the Hollywood blonde created in flesh, a kitsch game. And she used her looks to sell her music. Blondie's first single was promoted with a picture of pouting Debbie captioned 'Wouldn't you like to rip her to shreds?' Carefully posed photographs – often taken by her boyfriend, Chris Stein – were released to the press and the records duly charted. Then Debbie started to complain that people *believed* in this sex-goddess image.

Punk brought about a new awareness of image and manipulation. Singers such as Siouxsie and Pauline Murray (of Penetration) fought hard to be seen as part of a band rather than the focus; for a long time, the Banshees refused to be interviewed separately and resisted using pictures of

'Dayglo Adolescence': with her song lyrics and her costumes (a brilliant mix and match of synthetics and rejects), Poly Styrene spoke and dressed for a new generation of women resisting the roles on offer to them. (photo: Trevor Key)

themselves on record-sleeves or in press ads. The idea of women as equals, not to be unduly picked out in a group, persisted. By the time the shambolic, post-punk wave of bands began to make their presence felt, dressing-up on stage had all but gone. The Leeds girls, such as Mary of the Mekons, or Bethan Peters and Julz of Delta 5, wore much the same as the boys: dark, drab clothes and the omnipresent long, grey, mac. The Raincoats in London and the Au Pairs in Birmingham were equally careful about how women fitted into the structure of the four-piece band. No one took prominence in photographs and stage positions were considered carefully. The Raincoats experimented with swapping instrumental and lead vocal parts and both bands went through a phase of wearing 'street clothes'. The idea of not dressing any differently from the audience was central to the politics.

By 1979 the notion of a uniform 'youth' culture had burst apart: now there were definite 'tribes' – the skins, the mod revivalists, the punks, the rockers, and the heavy metal head-bangers. The trend that had preached (and practised) unity was 2-Tone, the logical result of the uneasy alliance between punk and reggae forged by the likes of Don Letts at the Roxy Club, Vivien Goldman in *Sounds*, and the enthusiastic Rock Against Racism groups everywhere. It was a style that also had some roots in 1960s multiracial line-ups – such as Blue Mink, who sang songs of racial harmony ('Melting Pot') and experimented with race images: singer Madeleine Bell braided and beaded her hair in African styles that were then rare in Britain.

Led by the Specials, 2-Tone had the energy of punk, the rhythm and tunes of ska, and sharp political comment. Pauline Black was one of the few women in the gang, and she dressed like the women in the audience – in Sta-Prest trousers, trilby, and a Harrington jacket. Rude Girls looked like Rude Boys.

Meanwhile, in the charts, the acceptable face of punk was asserting itself with women like Hazel O'Connor and Toyah Wilcox. Toyah mouthed rebellion and dressed it up in punky trappings (oh, so politely), while Hazel was

Hazel O'Connor's braids were a reaction to those executives who insisted she should keep the hairstyle she wore as Kate in 'Breaking Glass'. (photo: David Corio)

courted by the media in a love–hate relationship after her role in the film *Breaking Glass*.

Punk images had become rigid; outrage had been incorporated into fashion: models had shorter, cropped hair, wore more extreme make-up on some sessions, and scowled rather than smiled. Some feminists adopted the pretty-boy look – bright colours, spiky hair and Crazy Colour dyes – while the original punks became either more extreme with tattoos and mohicans, more and more ear-and nose-rings, or settled into small clubs and wine bars. In London, the focus was the Blitz Club. Punk was no longer outrageous, and 'style' was rediscovered by a generation in search of new costumes. Women once more became accessories, and the New Romantics were born.

It is significant that no new women equal to, say, Steve Strange or Boy George emerged from the cult. Perhaps Annabella LuWin, the 14-year-old girl 'discovered' by Malcolm McLaren in a laundrette, was the nearest thing – a woman with energy and charisma. Annabella, though, was dressed by Vivienne Westwood, sang lyrics written by McLaren, and fronted the band Bow Wow Wow put together without consultation with her. Her naked body – a publicity photo showed her draped only in a strip of tartan on a studio mixing-desk – helped sell the album, and her mother's objections only fuelled the fun.

IN THE PALACE OF THE VIDEO QUEENS

An emphasis on style and stereotypical good looks coincided with the rise of the video and the new pretty-boy pop of the 1980s. Women were once more expected to be unrealistically perfect, and were often reduced to fashion accessories again. The Human League claimed to have found two women, Suzanne Suley and Joanne Catherall, in a Sheffield disco and added them to their re-formed line-up on the basis that they simply looked good and could dance. The Fun Boy Three joined forces with the girly trio Bananarama to make glamorous videos and promote tracksuit chic.

As the video became an essential factor in the success of a single, more and more money was invested in production. From cheap promos of bands miming in glossy locations, they became fully fledged cinematic epics – sometimes even made by 'name' directors like Lindsay Anderson, who directed Carmel's video for 'More, More, More'. The success of the 24-hour music channel, MTV, in the USA and the advent of cable TV in Britain, means that the selling-power of the pop video is ever-increasing. Some bands are beginning to be signed on the strength of their image rather than their music, and songs are being written with the video in mind. The band become characters in the videos, switching and flicking roles like film actors.

The new emphasis on 'The Look' has meant that, more than ever, an image has to be carefully planned and chosen. Greater variety ironically results in more attention to image. So, instead of losing its tyranny, image continues to impose its expectations on all those who enter the world of pop music.

Today image is a far more self-conscious, well-thought-out creation. It is rarely taken literally, and there is no longer any need to dress in allegiance to a certain group all the time: a woman can dress in a psychedelic mini-skirt one day, go to a club in a ballgown the next, and wear dungarees and monkey boots the following morning. The past has been rifled for ideas since the 1960s. The old clothes that girls played with in dressing-up boxes as children are on sale in second-hand stores and flea markets everywhere. The world is the ragtrade's oyster, and different cultures are mixed and matched alongside different eras: African prints and Indian jewellery, Rasta hats and American baseball jackets . . . Anything goes, as long as it has style.

Annie Lennox
(photo: courtesy RCA Records)

CHAPTER TWO

WHAT SHALL

I

WEAR

?

SHERYL GARRATT & SUE STEWARD

'What shall I wear?' A question familiar to most of us as we rifle through our wardrobes to find the right outfit for a night out, a job interview or just a day at work. For performers, the pressure is much greater; their appearance is often scrutinized by thousands, picked over and criticized by the press. Of course, it's fun too: the opportunity to wear outrageous clothes, to hide behind masks of make-up – it can be like a grown-up dressing-up game. But a woman is faced with a sometimes bewildering number of elements and details. Dresses or trousers? What length skirt? How much of her body should she show? Male clothes are rarely as restrictive and never as symbolic as, say, a tight skirt and stiletto heels. Only in the small, private world of the urban gay scene are they used and interpreted as sexual symbols in the same way.

A woman on stage – whether she's wearing a side-split dress with a low-cut neck, or a casual street outfit – can expect to be assessed on the basis of her looks first, regardless of what she's doing. Each article of clothing carries its own associations, from leather fetish-wear to a woollen twinset. What at first seems spontaneous or trivial, often emerges in interviews to have more serious or interesting motives. Alannah Currie of the Thompson Twins wears outsize Foreign Legion/baseball hats which have become something of a trademark:

> I thought that the hat was really funny the first time I saw it. It's a totally practical thing, because I have long hair, and I didn't want to cut it off. On stage, I couldn't keep jumping around because when I started sweating, it all stuck to my face. And I've got blonde hair and I'm quite small and people have a certain attitude to small blondes. So I figured I should do something whereby I looked taller and bigger on stage, which would give me more power. The hat

works because it focuses attention away from my body, and they've started getting larger and more outrageous.

The political implications of clothes, are more and more evident: for instance, the Clash dress as macho commandos in order to tell their audiences to defy the state, or to stay out of the armed forces. And the agit-punk group, Crass, with their strident pacifist views, are even more extreme: wearing all-black, militaristic and menacing stage-clothes, they claim to be working with the contradictions of such an image, using it to attract the very audience they wish to influence. But their lyrics are inaudible live, and the lasting impression is one of violence and

Alannah Currie. (photo: Kerstin Rodgers)

masculinity. The Poison Girls toured extensively with Crass, building up their own following amongst hard punk and skinhead audiences. Vi Subversa explained their view of the situation:

> I personally feel that contradiction was a huge burden. No way did *we* want to appear military, but there was so much violence around that you had to wear fairly armoured clothes to feel safe. You couldn't wear open sandals when there were people maybe going to kick each other and you had to defend yourself – or run.

Practical considerations are another factor: clothes have to allow a performer to move on stage; for some women comfort is important, too. The strapless dress that keeps slipping paralyses many singers – Randy Crawford had an object lesson in what *not* to wear on stage as she shuffled to save herself from exposure. Comfort can also mean sheltering *behind* a look: wearing make-up like a mask, for instance. Dolly Parton is adept at disguise, fending off any prying into her 'real self' with her brilliant costumes and wigs.

The Slits were one of the few groups whose female members looked totally at ease and uninhibited on stage, wearing clothes that both looked 'feminine' and sensual, without becoming jailbait. Viv Albertine describes another common sartorial problem:

> One of the biggest things for me to work out – never having seen a woman on stage playing a guitar – was how to wear a skirt. I didn't know what length it should be, whether higher or lower than the guitar, what you should wear on your feet, how you should move now your skinny legs were hanging out the bottom of the guitar, instead of being covered by jeans which looks normal to the audience. You had to

The famed beehive of Neasden: Mari Wilson. (photo: David Corio)

change *their* ideas of what they'd seen and still hold their interest and admiration: That was all really hard.

COSTUME CHANGES

Clothes can be costumes for a narrative role: Lene Lovich built an eccentric character of mixed Eastern European and early Hollywood origins; Manhattan Transfer and Mari Wilson both simply recreated past eras (the 1940s and the 1960s). Though rare in pop music today, it used to be standard practice for the big dance bands and the 1960s all-girl groups all to wear identical costumes. Ivy Benson always dressed her 'girls' in the same outfits, regardless of their size and how well – or ill – they suited them, or their playing. Thirty years later, August Darnell, bandleader and musical director of Kid Creole and the Coconuts, selects the band's costumes. Carol Colman, who plays bass, accepts this as his prerogative:

> August makes all the decisions about wardrobe. We are cast like for a movie or a Broadway show. He writes my character in his play, then I have to get out there and do the part. On our first European tour, I had to leave off my 'khakis' which I'd always worn, and play in an authentic WAVE's [1940s naval officer] uniform – white skirt and high heels. I lay awake worrying about how I had to get on stage in that skirt and those high heels – not to mention my objection in the beginning to standing up to play! I had to *learn* how to stand up. But I wear those shoes all the time now, and sometimes have to stand for up to 90 minutes in the show.

From time to time, it has been argued that 'dressing down' – wearing street-clothes on stage – can actually lessen the gap between performer and audience. Some 1970s folk-rockers adopted this stance; punk rejected glamour and make-up as 'pop phenomena', unless they were used as a parody of a mask. Jordan's white face with its violet lightning-streak, or Siouxsie's black geometrical patterns were both OK, as they were outside of the beauty game – although, of course, the Siouxsie style soon filtered into mainstream good looks through fashion mags, models, and trade make-up lines.

For many people the Raincoats represented an inspiring match of theory and practice. But looking back to that period, Vicki Aspinall is careful to emphasize the difference between the media's version of their looks (dowdy feminists, and scruffy, serious girls) and how they saw themselves:

> We *did* have total disregard for glamour, but it was misrepresented by the media equation of feminists as humourless, dowdy and dull stereotypes. We thought a lot about what to wear on stage, and enjoyed dressing-up for gigs, but it wasn't a conventionally glamorous style.

Sadly, it isn't only the media who show a blinkered attitude towards women on stage. Lesley Woods, singer and guitarist with the Au Pairs, suffered criticisms about her stage appearance:

> I remember getting into several arguments with women about whether a feminist can wear make-up. As far as I'm concerned, feminism gives women the chance to express themselves *for* themselves, not to be subjected by the rules and values imposed by living in a male-dominated society. It must go beyond the line that women who wear make-up are making themselves fodder for men.

What was being demanded was that Lesley dress down, and hide her body and her looks *for political reasons*.

Some black women refuse to go along with the options open to them. For years, A & M records have had to contend with Joan Armatrading's resilient determination *not* to conform to *any* stereotypes. She maintains a very low-key stage and publicity image – blouses and T-shirts with jeans – and promotion shots have had, therefore, to look to other ways of offering her visually.

'We are Frank Chickens':
Kazumi Taguchi (left), Kazuko Hohki (right).
(photo: Richard Rowland, courtesy KAZ Records)

Publicity shots generally tend to be studio fantasies, giving little or no information about the artist's talent or work, and it is interesting that Joan is treated differently – she is often shown playing guitar.

COLOUR RULES
Black and Asian women working in what is still a predominantly white industry face different choices about what to wear, dictated by both the

stereotypes imposed on them by whites, and by the ideas about women in their own culture. The Japanese duo Frank Chickens, for example, live in London partly to escape the restraint of their homeland: 'As foreigners, we don't feel we have to conform.' In their act, they play with Western ideas of the Japanese, the role of women in Japanese society, the old (Geishas and Samurais) and the new (Walkman stereos and Godzilla). 'By using stereotypes, we can break through them and show who we really are.' So, in 'Yellow Toast':

> *Oh, we like being foreign Nips*
> *Because you all think we are hip*
> *But if you think we are so wise*
> *Why don't you look us in the eyes?*
>
> *All the men love the yellow woman*
> *You think our mother taught us sin*
> *And yellow sex is just amazing.*
>
> *If you are happy with the illusion*
> *And you want to have no conclusion*
> *Oh, we love England green and free*
> *We think this is the place to be.'*

For disco star Nazia Hassan, the problems were reversed: she was brought up in England from the age of five, and when she and her brother suddenly became stars in India through one song on a film soundtrack album (recorded in London), she was faced with a bewildering set of new conventions:

Images in India are totally stereotyped. You can't be normal people. Singers are either goddesses or vamps; all the Indian actresses who play the goody-goody in films are the goody-goody off-screen as well; only the Westernized actresses – good looking, good figures, that sort of thing – are supposed to have 'fast lives'. Film singers are supposed to be very 'good': Lata Mangeshkar's image

Sheila Chandra: ambassador of Indi-pop.
(photo: courtesy Mobile Suit Corporation)

Almost unwittingly, the Hassans shattered the stereotypes that had held true in India for many years, challenging the assumptions about Western music and dress which had previously been taken to indicate loose morals. They also introduced disco into a pop music that had previously consisted entirely of film soundtracks sung by veterans such as Lata Mangeshkar.

When British-born actress Sheila Chandra tried for the UK charts with the Indi-pop group, Monsoon, she projected an entirely different image to a public who still largely saw Indian dress as exotic. She was an opulent exaggeration of Western ideas of the East, looking like a Turkish delight ad, in richly coloured saris, dark eye make-up and wearing (along with the men in the band) a red dot in the middle of the forehead.

is that she doesn't drink, doesn't care about money, and prays every day. Because we'd done a fast pop song, we were told we have to be zany and gregarious. We just said, 'We're just going to be what we are, and if you don't like it, tough.' I strode around in jeans because that's what I wore here, I wasn't going to change. At that stage, I used to wear dungarees and I was trying to grow my hair, so it was in pigtails all the time. I didn't use any make-up – only a little bit of lip-gloss when my father wasn't looking. We never tried to be 'Westernized' or 'Eastern', just what we were. I think that's what made us popular in India. A few people did complain because we were too Westernized, but then I suppose people started to realize that it didn't mean you *had* to be bad. I think the critics were silenced by the majority when everybody turned around and said, 'They're just good kids.'

Nigerian musician Fela Kuti uses his wives as exotic trappings of his live shows. (photo: Stella Whalley)

40

The Lijadu Sisters, Kehinde and Taiwo, two forceful Nigerian singers who maintain their traditional looks while strongly rejecting their traditional roles. (photo: Harcourt films)

This kind of exotic packaging is a seductive marketing ploy – another stereotype for women to be shaped by.

Notions of exotica do change, of course. What is exotic in one culture can be commonplace and everyday somewhere else. Possibly because of his prolonged stays in the USA and London, the Nigerian politician/pop star Fela Kuti understands the effects of calculated 'exotica' on Western audiences, and wilfully exaggerates and exploits it. Fela's travelling show includes a handful of his 27 wives ('Queens') as singers and dancers. Several of them have worked as Paris fashion models, and they look exquisite: their painted and made-up faces and beaded hair designs combine traditional styles with a dash of Parisian elegance. They are the focus of the band,

even though they only appear a few times ... led on stage by one of the band, they split up and dance on one spot, a hypnotic, hip-swivelling routine. *But* ... they are deliberately used by Fela: in their tiny mini-skirts and bikini tops, their function is indistinguishable from that of exotic go-go dancers in Western night-clubs – and they're a long way from being the envoys of Yoruba culture that Fela pretends.

The pop music coming into Britain from African countries reveals that the majority of female artists are singers. And like most people in urban areas of Africa, they sometimes wear traditional clothes, sometimes Western. It is predictable that those singers working with soul and disco-derived material (Nigeria's Dora Ifudu and Christie Essaien) go for the same lip-glossed looks, and sparkly dresses, T-shirts and trousers, as their counterparts in the States. Some, like Nigerian Queen Selawa Abeni, wear loose, traditional gowns and sometimes head-dresses, too, for their performances of neo-traditional music. The 18-piece (all policewomen) Les Amazones de Guinée (Guinea) wear vibrant dresses in local prints whose styles, like their music, reveal signs of Western influence. Ironically, when African stars come to play in the West, the audiences tend to want them to look 'African': they expect exotica, and that is exactly what Fela Kuti provides through 'his women'.

For black women living in Western culture, the problems are different. They have to contend with the dominant notion that their sexuality is somehow less inhibited, more animalistic, than that of white women. Tina Turner's 1984 tour was publicized through a huge poster showing her rushing towards the camera, in a skirt made from animal furs, with tails hanging from her waist. The caption reads: 'Captured live . . . Tina

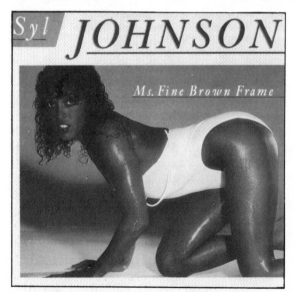

A composite of male sexual fantasies about black women.
(Sleeve courtesy Epic Records)

Turner'. Mr Syl Johnson's hit soul record 'Ms Fine Brown Frame' featured this kind of imagery, while Grace Jones was once portrayed in a publicity picture on all-fours, caged and snarling at the viewer.

But this can be used to the artist's advantage. One male reviewer said he felt 'emasculated' by Millie Jackson's unrelenting attack on male sexual prowess. Disco-singer Sharon Redd also uses her stage performances to twist expectations in a positive way: men who made advances during her show at a London gay club, Bolts, were taken up on their offers with such gusto that they withdrew whimpering! Whether such tactics would work outside the gay scene is another question. Indeed, it is interesting that most of the performers who are sexually explicit, potentially threatening to male egos, or a challenge to conventional ideas of femininity or female beauty, perform mainly on the (male) gay circuit. Both Grace Jones and Bette Midler started their singing careers on the gay scene where their 'outrageousness' was more acceptable and many, such as Laura Pallas, remain there. In fact, a whole genre – 'Hi-energy', created especially for the gay market – involves women singing sexually assertive songs such as Miquel Brown's 'So Many Men, So Little Time'.

An alternative is to avoid this sexualization altogether. 'Dignity' is a word that recurs again and again in interviews with black women working in all fields of music. Probably most successful in reshaping perceptions of black women performers was the 'African Queen' image. Adopted by both the black Muslim movement in the US and the Rastafarians, this reinvented image of Africa is exemplified by Bob Marley's backing group, the I-Threes: long, flowing, brightly coloured dresses cover the body, wrapped turbans and scarves cover the head, creating a sensual and beautiful appearance without appearing as mere fodder for male

The I-Threes, here at rehearsal for a Bob Marley and the Wailers show. (photo: Dennis Morris)

fantasies. It can be restrictive, though. Soul singer Ruby Turner described how she eventually tired of the look, reverting instead to clothes closer to her everyday self, an office-worker from Birmingham. However, the new image was still, she stressed, 'dignified'. Though English lovers'-rock singers favour a similar style of sophisticated, everyday clothes, a new breed of British reggae singers is emerging. Led by Sister Audrey and Ranking Ann and Shani Benjamin, they wear mainly army-surplus gear, like their male counterparts; their tough, militant look is matched by strong lyrics that attack both racism *and* sexism. It is certainly an exciting new direction.

STAY AS SWEET AS YOU ARE

Pop music, so the story goes, is made by the young for the young. But one look at the charts will usually debunk the myth, with the likes of Queen, Billy Joel and Diana Ross regularly waving the flag for the over-thirties. In reality, both the producers and the consumers are older than the market would like to acknowledge. The myth persists because it is profitable: as rock'n'roll limps into its fourth decade, producers don baseball caps to pretend they're not balding, the Stones continue to believe they are making music for 'the kids', and everyone politely ignores the fact that Rod, Mick and Cliff aren't 20 any more. Rock is about rebellion, the generation gap, Real Men and fast chicks, and although these horny old myths are dying, there's still no room for people who admit to being old, and look it. For women, especially, age is an important factor – men become more 'distinguished' with the years, while women 'decay'.

Given the pop world's emphasis on looks, a woman moving into her fourth decade is, simply, not on. Now that Debbie Harry has crossed the line, she is candid about her fears and is attempting to create a new career for herself as an actress. But it is only mainstream, Western pop and rock which sets such a premium on youth. For jazz aristocrats like Sarah Vaughan and Ella Fitzgerald, age and reputations are seen as proof of authenticity and skill: a link with the music's history, respected almost like vulnerable museum-pieces. 'I'm glad I saw her before she dies,' breathed one Nina Simone fan at her season at Ronnie Scott's club in London in early 1984. Ms Simone is just 50.

Most other kinds of popular music have their own hierarchies where older women influence and entertain audiences of all ages and are often powerful enough to stop successors until *they* decide it is time to step down. India's most idolized star, for example, is the film soundtrack singer Lata Mangeshkar, a woman well into her sixties. Her voice is usually associated with the younger, attractive actresses who mime to its sound on screen (indeed, Mangeshkar only took up singing when smallpox marked her face and made an acting career impossible). She is, nevertheless, respected as a performer. On her rare visits to Britain, her concerts sell out to old and young alike, huge audiences wearing everything from saris to disco-gear. Celia Cruz,

For the salsa world, there is only one female star: Celia Cruz. Her audience includes her contemporaries as well as passionate fans two generations down.   (photo: courtesy *Latin NY*, by Jimmy Arruaz)

New York's Queen of salsa and madonna of the city's thriving Latin dance music, is again a woman old enough to be collecting a pension in the UK. Incredibly, her career stretches from pre-Castro night-clubs in 1940s Havana to Madison Square Gardens in the 1980s. Her fans include her own exiled contemporaries as well as young inhabitants of electro-New York who have never even seen Cuba. Then there is the Cajun accordion-player Queen Ida, who didn't begin performing until her children had grown up and left home. Every year, she brings her stuttering, exuberant Louisiana music to England accompanied by a band young enough to *be* her kids.

These examples are a curious non-rock phenomenon: they are integral to the pop music of their own cultures, but none share the attitudes to age that permeate the rock industry.

So what *does* happen to old rock stars? Though rock is a relatively new genre, already there are familiar routes for women who are either bored with the fast changes of pop charting, or whose days of chart success are over. The more versatile – such as Cilla Black and Lulu – have found their niches in variety entertainment. Combining comedy, singing, dancing, and chatting to guests, they host standard TV family shows, work the seaside shows in summer, and do pantomimes at Christmas. Their fans are largely people of the same age who remember them as bright young stars on *Ready Steady Go!* and who, like the stars themselves, now have families and mortgages, too.

For those who prefer to keep singing as their main focus, there are the working-men's clubs, cabarets, and night-clubs, and for the lucky few, such as Shirley Bassey, the international Las Vegas-style circuit. Helen Shapiro was shunted on to the club circuit because there was nowhere else to go, as were Susan Maugham, Kathy Kirby, and other stars of the pre-Beatles charts. Ousted by the likes of Sandie Shaw and Marianne Faithfull, Helen found herself a has-been at the tender age of 21:

> As far as I was concerned, I never had an image, but people kept this old image of me which started to work against me. I was out of date, and I couldn't get on to the shows because I wasn't current or relevant. I found it very frustrating, and I got very depressed for a time. Luckily, I got out of it and now this new interest in the 1960s means that I'm flavour of the month – 22 years on!

Sandie Shaw herself was soon pushed out on

Queen Ida's catchy Cajun music attracts audiences throughout Europe. (photo: Pam Isherwood/Format)

or style her costumes should be:

> Just before I put the BEF record out ['Music of Quality and Distinction'], I'd started going to the clubs and girls would lock me in the toilets till I told them my beauty secrets! But they were stuck in a time-warp. I thought, 'I'm different now, but on the other hand, I'm not super-trendy any more.' And coming back was hard, because you have to have an image now, especially if you're a woman. Before, I'd just thought it was 'natural', and I felt I should approach it that way this time, too. It's all so irrelevant to me to spend so much time on what I look like. It's important to be presentable, though, for the make-up to be right when the light hits. That's professional.

Perhaps of all the 1960s women still around, only Tina Turner and Joni Mitchell have come close to the Dorian Grey quality apparently achieved by the old men of rock. After the break with her husband, Ike, Tina Turner persevered with a solo career and finally charted again with a cover of Al Green's 'Let's Stay Together' (another BEF production). But she is tolerated *in spite of* her age, as well as *because of* the pedigree it gives her. She is still sold in the same terms as her younger sisters – looking their age, too, with her blonde wig, super-fit body, and costumes which reveal her still shapely trademark, her thighs. Joni Mitchell, on the other hand, has maintained a consistently comfortable elegance, the style of a wealthy, independent woman. She escapes pop pundits' age prejudice because she's respected as more than 'just a singer' and, being judged on her musical merits, manages to carry an audience of more than her contemporaries.

Vi Subversa, singer and guitarist with the Poison Girls, broke far more taboos than either Tina Turner or Joni Mitchell: she *began* at 40. In 1975 Vi was singing in public for the first time,

Tina Turner's image stereotypes black women as wild and fascinating for their dangerous, threatening sexuality.
(photo: Kerstin Rodgers)

to the same marginal track, until the arrival of 1980s nostalgia and two recording appearances – first with British Electric Foundation (BEF) and, more recently, with the Smiths. While Helen Shapiro came back with the jazz and blues standards she'd always preferred, wearing the slightly formal, classic clothes she likes, Sandie Shaw hovers around the edges of current pop, unsure whether to jump in – or what colour looking – apart from her clothes and 'Crazy-coloured' hair – like the middle-aged mother she was. It was a shock, even during the heady, politically aggressive, late 1970s. She, more than anyone, has confronted audiences with their false assumptions about age:

> Well, we were old, let's face it! We must have looked like their mums and aunties and social workers: authority figures getting in on their act. But it didn't take long to break that down, and there's a lot of affection that keeps us going now.
>
> I think ageism is as terrible as sexism, in the sense that the dividing-line separates people from each other. The sexual game that goes on between women and men means that at least they talk to each other and are involved in each other's lives. But older and younger people just split off more and more: there's no basis for dialogue most of the time.

The pop press, which is managed mostly by people older than its readers, find this aspect of the Poison Girls difficult to cope with:

> NME (New Musical Express) deals with us at the end of tongs from time to time. Obviously we're not a number one Smash Hits band, but the odd feature could go in, nevertheless. There's huge resistance to us on that level. They've actually said, 'Oh, but the kids don't want to see older women.' And they quote letters from their young fans, which is precisely why we ought to be in there. The barriers of ageism and sexism are connected in that not only am I older, I am also female.

Last word to Millie Jackson, mistress of sex and soul. Her most recent trip to England (she was 39 at the time) prompted the same question in almost every interview: 'How long can you keep on doing this?' As long as her plastic surgeon's skill allows, she joked. More seriously, she added that she would probably drop half of her band and work as a comedy act. She had a line ready for that day: 'Is there any of you young folks out there can do it now like I used to do?'

THE FAT AND THE THIN OF IT

Size, like age, has always been a determining factor in pop music: big women are usually considered ugly, unfashionable, and are unlikely to be featured in magazines or on TV. To succeed, they must have an 'outsize' personality to compensate for their lack of conventional good looks, so the argument goes, and they must also have the self-confidence to be able to cope with comments, jokes and criticisms about their size.

For women, especially, this can be difficult as weight gains and losses are often connected with emotional problems. Women in the public eye – from Lady Di to Debbie Harry – are under much greater pressure and more constant scrutiny than the rest of us. In the 1970s, Mama Cass died tragically early from a heart attack. Her enormous size had been a public admission of her inability to cope with fame, fortune and the lifestyle of a rock star. On the other side of that coin, US singer Karen Carpenter died at the age of 32 of a heart attack induced by years of strain from anorexia. And at this moment, Lena Zavaroni, a British child star dragged into international fame from the age of 10 and deprived of a normal childhood or adolescence, spends much of her life in hospital trying to conquer anorexia and to become easy with herself, her fame, and, particularly, her body.

Tragic stories of women's quest to look the right size dominate the pop world. A star is never allowed to forget that she has an image to live up to: when Debbie Harry posed for the cover of Blondie's Parallel Lines album, for instance, there were snide comments in the press implying that

she was wearing a dress because she'd put on weight.

'Before I was well known,' comments singer Helen Terry, 'people on building-sites would say, "Look at the state of her, the fat cow." They don't do that any more because they think they recognize me, but now what happens is that the so-called educated women and men of the press have taken up the role of building-site hecklers. It's a really simplistic mentality, and it annoys me that it makes something I'm singing so much less worth while than it should be.' Helen Terry did not appear in the promo-video for Culture Club's 'It's a Miracle' – even though she sang a long solo on the single. Who *did* appear? A slim blonde, go-go dancer in a pair of Union Jack shorts.

Some of the most positive statements about size have come from black women performers, perhaps because large women are still, to some extent, prized in black communities, and con- sidered attractive, sexual beings. In Jamaica, for instance, the drug Anarexol is sold for girls whose men don't like them skinny. In his song 'Anarexol', DJ Eek-a-mouse is perplexed by the growing size of his girlfriend: is it Anarexol or the man who sends her letters every day? The idols of jazz, blues and gospel music have often been large women, wearing loose, voluminous gowns. Male Afro-American and Caribbean singers often exhort their women to 'put some flesh on their bones' and extol the virtues of a 'fatty bum bum'.

In an interview with *She* magazine, singer Bertice Reading announced: 'You have to have confidence in the fact that you are big. Get it right out of your mind that you ought to be thin. If you are comfortable *and* healthy and your weight is not bothering you physically, why

should it bother you mentally? Dress well, fix yourself up, and just go out there and hit 'em!' Even so, Ms Reading still has problems when looking for attractive clothes to fit her: 'I don't want to look like an upholstered armchair or a floral tent or a house on fire.'

American disco duo, the Weather Girls, make their size into a joke which they then confound with their brilliant records. As Two Tons of Fun, they worked as backing singers with the chubby transvestite Sylvester, and all three delighted in mocking their sizes, and singing within the same range – Sylvester in falsetto, the Two Tons inhabiting those middle and upper realms of the best gospel-soul singers. They are regarded with affection, but also as camp, and kitsch; adored by gay male audiences, but not considered as real sexual beings. But their 1984 album, *Success*, continues their positive, confident self- advertisements:

> Playboy *offered us our weight in gold,*
> *They'd better add some pages to the*
> *centrefold.*
> *'Cause we're the biggest, we're the best*
> *Most beautiful, glamorous, fabulous girls in*
> *the world.*

Nevertheless, the stereotype of the fat, happy black woman is a dangerous one, an heir of the distorted Hollywood image of thigh-slapping, eye-rolling, laughing black mamas.

'DON'T CALL ME NO ENGLISH GIRL'
When Pauline Black interviewed Millie Jackson for Channel 4's *Black on Black* show, she asked the singer – who writes, publishes and produces her own material, as well as managing herself – whether it was still as hard for women to manage their own affairs. The reply was abrupt and unexpected: 'I hate to burst your bubble, dear,' she smiled, and explained that race, not gender is the main problem. 'Look at the budget for a white

Izora Armstead and Martha Walsh, once known as Two Tons of Fun, now the Weather Girls, are grandmothers who gleefully break the rules about age and size. (photo: Kerstin Rodgers) rock band, and look at the budget for an r'n'b artist – and you'll be completely startled at the difference in the figures.' For black women working in a predominantly white culture, racism often remains a far greater problem than sexism.

Black women are even less visible than their white equivalents because of the small amounts of money allocated to the promotion of black music. Racism – usually disguised as a preference for (white) pop or rock – keeps black acts generally from the radio, press and TV, and further disadvantages black women. Disco and dance-floor music, the most commercially successful music made by mainly black artists, rarely relies on the cult of the personality. Its singers are almost anonymous, disappearing from view after the personal appearances to promote their one-off hit; fans are more likely to collect records by the same producer than the same singer, the mix being where the strength of a dance single usually lies. Potentially, this could give black women more freedom from the unwritten rule that female performers should be young, slim, and conventionally pretty. In reality, however, black woman have to be *even more* glamorous than their white sisters to be accepted by the companies or the media, as well as having to meet expectations exclusive to their colour. The double bind is summed up by Pauline Black:

Blacks are still playing to the archetype that the white man has of them, and in a lot of ways, yes, you can dress it up in all sorts of fancy dances, body-popping, and all the rest of it, but it's still the kind of tap-dancing, 'roll your eyeballs for them' job. It's still not you being there and being real because that threatens them. They can't handle that. Most of the black women I know at the moment are conforming to that in one way or another. I probably am,

too, but I'm not sure to what. I'll have to find out. That attitude is just as prevalent amongst blacks as whites – the lighter you are, the better it is. If you're being as white as possible, it's the icing on the cake for record companies.

It is impossible to 'transcend' colour. The artist cannot become magically transparent or raceless, only *white*. 'Diana Ross is no longer a black girl,' noted Marcia Gillespie bitterly in an article on the Supremes in *Ms* magazine. 'She is a superstar.' And, sure enough, there is Diana on the cover of her album, *Silk*, looking as white as Reagan himself. But it is, of course, only honorary whitedom: the dubious 'privilege' can be withdrawn at any time. Once black artists *do*, against all odds, 'cross over' to a bigger audience, their fight becomes one of remaining black.

Militancy is not welcomed, and women such as Nina Simone and Eartha Kitt paid dearly for their involvement in the 1960s liberation movements. There were, however, gains as well as casualties: in the USA, LaBelle, Sly and the Family Stone, and the Parliament/Funkadelic/Parlet Corporations explored new images of black performers, while black women everywhere discovered the afro, braiding and beading. In the UK and the Caribbean, Rastafarians brought dreadlocks into fashion. In the 1980s, black hair is still hidden under wigs and hats, talent remains hidden by a racist notion of 'natural rhythm' and black women, particularly, are dogged by the idea of insatiable, animal sexuality – an image designed to keep them one rung down from that more restrained, civilized place on the ladder reserved for whites. Popular music, like the society that produces it, is both racist and sexist.

GIRLS AND BOYS COME OUT TO PLAY
In the past few years, a new option has emerged for women: the media and fans have become

obsessed with androgyny. At the end of 1983, kiddiepop mag *Smash Hits* featured Annie Lennox and (Boy) George O'Dowd, on its cover. Both wore identical make-up and begged the question (though we all knew the answer), 'Which one is the boy?' 'The Genderbenders', the *Sun* called them in a rare moment of wit. In January 1984, *Woman* magazine (which had already run features on George and Marilyn) called Annie 'seemingly hermaphrodite'. Male and female at the same time?

Symptomatic of the confusion that surrounds sexual roles at the moment, androgyny reflects the longings of both sexes (whether acknowledged or not) to incorporate elements of the other. Now, more than ever, we are aware of the restrictions and the advantages suffered or enjoyed by both sexes. Now more than ever, we know that 'natural's not in it'. And whether appalled or infatuated, attracted or repelled,

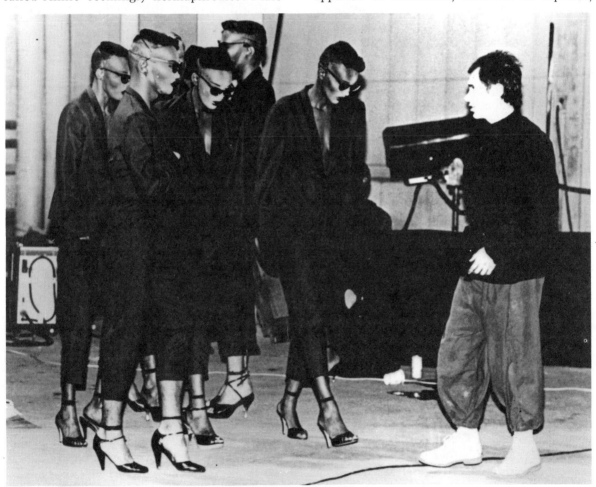

'One-man show': Grace Jones clones prepare to make their entry, under the direction of stylist Jean-Paul Goude.
(photo: courtesy Island Pictures)

everyone wants to know about the few that play with the rules and our fantasies. Gamine Annie and pretty Boy George were the faces of 1983, and more could be added to the list. Grace Jones is playing a Zulu Warrior in *Conan II*, co-starring with Arnold Schwarzenegger, himself a gross exaggeration of masculinity. Michael Jackson, the biggest star the world has ever known, has gone to great lengths – even surgery – to look as feminine as possible. There was a girl called Alf, and a boy named Marilyn.

By dressing as a man, a woman can also gain their (relative) freedom and power. Neither the insight nor the activity is new, of course. Murray Hall died in 1901. A respected American politician for 30 years, he married twice, and it was not until his death that his secret was discovered: he was a woman. Women weren't allowed to *vote* at that time, let alone stand for government; lesbians were not given even the little space they have today.

Few of us are willing to go as far as Murray Hall, and completely give up our female identity. But dressing like a man has a safe place and a long tradition in show biz: from the English music hall stars like Vesta Tilley and Ella Shields in their men's suits, silver canes and white carnations, to Annie Lennox, in her steel-grey suit and boxing boots. The point about the current vogue, however, is that we *know* it's a game. Marilyn, who once wore dresses and did, at times, look very much like Monroe, chose to make his *Top of the Pops* debut in more subtle garb: satin trousers, shirt open to show his nipples and so his gender to anyone who cared to look closely; George opts for smocks not frocks. Both have so far been careful to be ambiguous about their sexuality. Cuddly Mad Hatter George proclaims that he'd rather have a cup of tea, anyway, cleverly rendering himself safe, sanitized and cute. Lennox takes care, too, to balance her images, never leaving any doubt as to her true sexual identity. In the 'Who's That Girl?' video, butch-boy Annie is countered with Annie in a long blonde wig, *the femme fatale*.

Only Grace Jones plays it almost for real. In her 'One-Man Show' at Drury Lane in 1982 during 'Pull Up To The Bumper' (a song full of sexual innuendo), she dragged a man out of the audience and simulated anal sex with him. Grace the Man can also be homosexual. Which can be seen as either the ultimate expression of masculinity, or the ultimate threat to it, depending on where you stand in the sexual debate. Even though you know she's a woman, there's still something abnormal in her taking the dominant ('masculine') role. She is threatening, aggressive (and black), which is why the media were never as attracted to her as they were to Lennox or O'Dowd. Grace is acting the part of a *man*, not a boy; Clint Eastwood rather than Depeche Mode. She's also drawing on the long history of 'women as men' in her choice of images: in the same show, she made her entrance in a gorilla suit, moving on stage for a while before yanking off the head to reveal herself – a shock. But not for those who had seen Marlene Dietrich do exactly the same in *Blonde Venus*, 50 years earlier. Dietrich was the woman who brought trousers to Hollywood and, in the same film, sang a number dressed in a white tuxedo. Also, the idea of playing an opposite has racial as well as sexual significance for Grace. Interviewed by Kristine McKenna in NME in 1983, she mused, 'I've always had this kind of image that's allowed me to pass the colour barrier, and I have an idea for a film where I could play a white girl . . . it would be similar to de Niro's gaining weight for *Raging Bull* – I like the political implications of that.'

Androgyny became high fashion, though, in the 1960s, when the likes of Twiggy put breasts and bums out of style and made the ideal body pre-pubescent, childlike and asexual. Long hair and denims for both sexes brought further ambiguity, although it wasn't until the advent of Roxy Music, Bowie and glam-rock that such images became commonplace in music. In the mid-1970s, a boyishly free but inescapably feminine image held sway, epitomized in Julie Covington's role in the TV series, *Rock Follies*.

Androgynous images can give freedom to a female performer, allowing her to avoid the criteria usually used to judge women on stage by focusing attention away from her body. Pauline Black tells why, when her band the Selecter became part of the 2-Tone craze, she chose to dress in the same clothes as the men involved, and why she later reverted to wearing dresses on stage:

It was basically a defence. The guys were into wearing that style of clothes, and there was no way I wanted to go on stage looking, if you like, like 'A Girl'. So I wandered round the shops in Leicester and got myself a rather neat little suit, which I quite liked. I donned the hat because I didn't know what to do with my hair, and decided that I felt quite good. The first gig I did that way, nobody knew whether I was a boy with a high voice, or a girl who's a bit of a dyke, but once it became established that that was the way I dressed, then it was all right.

We looked exactly as if we knew what we were talking about, we knew what we were into, and that was that. But then by 1981, the music had started to change, and I'd started to sing more than in the early days, and I just began *feeling* different. My hair had started growing, so I thought I'd try wearing a dress and see what happened. And it was all right. It didn't seem to set off any reaction, so I had a go at wearing dresses for a bit. I just felt it was time that you could go out and perform as 'A Girl' and

be seen as 'A Girl', I suppose.

It must be remembered, though, that this option is open only to women with the bodies to fit it. Perhaps this is why there are not thousands of Lennox clones, despite her popularity. Annie Lennox is a fantasy figure for most women and girls. She is powerful, free to move and to be up on stage with the boys; she is also vulnerable-looking, fragile and beautiful. Able to be loved.

There's yet another new style emerging for women, and the image is already filtering into music: muscles. Perhaps this is the first trend with the potential to offer a real, rather than an illusory, gain in power. On the cover of the Eurythmics *Touch* LP, Annie Lennox is shown flexing her arm (although maybe the joke is in her assuming such a male pose when her arms are so fragile). Grace Jones is a Zulu Warrior; Carol Kenyon's first single, 'Warrior Woman', was promoted with a picture of the former session-singer releasing a falcon with a strong, well-developed arm. The strong-woman option is one that is open to all women – not just those with sculpted faces and waiflike figures – and may, in the 1980s, prove to be the basis for women to realize their own autonomy *as women*.

MARKETING VALUES

Once an artist has chosen a look (or had it chosen for her) it must be packaged and sold to the public. The rules of marketing apply as much to a record as to an underarm deodorant, and the original intention can often be horribly distorted in the process. A public image is built up, like an identikit drawing, from the kaleidoscope of visual images (photographs, record-sleeves and, increasingly, videos); the written word also remains a powerful tool in constructing the portrait of the artist. The artist has little chance to affect the 'angle' required by journalists. There is no way of presenting or receiving a neutral

From the androgyny of her earlier 2-Tone days, Pauline Black was persuaded into a glamour image when she went solo.
(photo: courtesy London Weekend Television)

The record company seemed to feel, 'Well, she's gone solo, we'll make her wear dresses and get some Brian Aris photos done of her.' I was very disorientated at the time about what I wanted to do, and I was getting sucked into something that just wasn't me. I spent another year trying to put it all back together again.

After being persuaded to record a cover version of 'Shoo Rah, Shoo Rah' (which she didn't like), and appear on the sleeve carefully posed and exposed, Pauline Black reasserted herself. She is now working as a TV presenter for Channel 4's *Black on Black*. Recent press photos showed her dressed in a tracksuit, relaxed, happy and strong. But are all women as lucky?

The standards imposed on women are impossibly high. The rules and restrictions of what is acceptable are much more rigid than for men, though men do sometimes experience similar bullying – especially in this mid-1980s phase of dewy-eyed, pretty pop boys. They can contend with it by the fact that they possess more of a sense of self *outside* their bodies. On the whole, what they actually *do* is taken into consideration; women, on the other hand, are taught that the most important thing is how to *look*. To criticize or remodel a woman's appearance often also affects both her ideas about herself and how others perceive her. It is far harder for a woman to take off her image when she goes home at night.

Finally, because both the media *and* the music industry are still seen to be dominated by men, there is a tendency to see female artists as male creations. So with Grace Jones: just as her music is often seen solely as a product of Sly Dunbar's and Robbie Shakespeare's virtuosity, her image is frequently described as the creation of her photographer and ex-lover, Jean-Paul Goude – a claim which Grace Jones herself vehemently

impression: the picture on a page represents the final stage of a chain-reaction involving photographer, picture editor, designers, record company and advertising agency marketing executives and – sometimes – the performer, as well. Theoretically, this team is there to sell more product – records; in practice, they are selling more than that – a package-deal identity of the artist, regardless of how she sees herself.

When the Selecter split up and Pauline Black went solo, her overall image also underwent a significant change:

refutes.

But, from Alma Cogan and her hand-sewn creations to Toyah Wilcox's chameleon-like identity changes, there have always been women who've colluded in the creation of their images. The results may not reflect how they want to look or how they appear in private; they do reflect the artist's awareness of what will help sell her product. Sheena Easton works closely with make-up artists and with photographer Brian Aris to produce images appropriate to her latest release – from (modern) 'girl next door' to sophisticated James Bond lady. Alannah Currie of the Thompson Twins not only controls her own image, but also that of the two men in the band. Such autonomy doesn't always pay off in terms of record sales – and this is presumably one reason why the 'experts' are reluctant to relinquish control to the artist. The cover of the Slits' first LP, *Cut*, showed the three women half-naked and coated in mud. It brought shrieks from all corners. The Slits were naively shocked by the reaction, as Viv Albertine remembers:

Nobody could see the strength, the joke, the little twist that we were all a bit fat. They were thinking we were trying a come on and sell our image. What would they prefer – us all dolled up in something fashionable? We wanted to write songs that wouldn't go out of fashion and we felt that about the cover, too. We didn't expect to have to explain it! But in the end, everything we did solidified our image; you get a lot of shit for not fitting into a box. And gradually we had to accept that we weren't going to shake off the Slits' *Wild Women of Wongo* image. No A&R men were interested in us for a long time, and even when we signed to CBS, we still couldn't get the radio DJs to relent on their opinion of us.

Since the new awareness and emphasis on artistic control introduced by punk, artists have been increasingly involved in their own marketing. The problems of control for women continue, however. The Slits' LP cover was still too ambiguous and subversive for the market, and they suffered for it. Some changes to women's images have more serious implications. When Judy Mowatt's album *African Woman* was released in Jamaica, its status as a militant call for liberation was reflected in the Rastafarian Twelve Tribes cover symbolism; Island Records replaced this with a muted glamour portrait, taking Mowatt's music out of the political context of her Rasta beliefs.

Even the most independent artists often find they have to play the marketing game. Carroll Thompson is a lovers'-rock (reggae) singer who writes, publishes and produces her own material, which is released through her own production company. Her first album, *Hopelessly in Love*, was clearly a low-budget and quite amateur production; the second came in a glossy, more expensive sleeve with a more glamorous photograph – and, soon after, *Hopelessly in Love*, was repackaged in the same way.

If we want to get across to a larger audience, then we have to compete at their level. We found that to really push it in the right direction, we would have to spend some money and we decided to do that because it's all part of the game. I just do the pictures and then forget it, because it doesn't have to be your true, everyday self. Some people live up to the image all the time – they go down the street the same as they look on their album covers. I don't because that's not how I *am* all the time, I can't bear to be like that.

The new independent labels of the mid-1970s were no better in their handling and treatment of female artists than the majors they criticized.

When the Adverts signed to Stiff Records, bassist Gaye Advert had posed for photos wearing a coat. The pictures that actually appeared showed her head superimposed on a naked body. Stiff compounded the insult when promoting the single: Gaye was offered as the prize to the sales rep who sold most copies of the record. 'That was a joke,' Gaye said afterwards. 'I wasn't going to actually do anything. I got £10 for it, and a free LP, too.'

Women's bodies are used to sell their own music in the same way they are used to sell records made by men, guitars, hi-fi speakers, and any other consumer item. It is expected of them. And women such as Siouxsie of the Banshees, who first refused to be featured on her record-sleeves or advertisments, now toe the line. It is not always a simple case of flesh-baring for sexually inviting pictures: sometimes it is more subtle – simply being there is enough. Hence, the appeal of having a woman in the group.

TRADE SECRETS

There is, of course, no way of giving a neutral visual picture of a performance: even with live photos, which can be assumed to show an artist looking more 'natural' than posed studio shots, the preconceptions of others intervene. Photographers choose which shots – out of several rolls of film – to print up and offer to the press, then the picture editor selects which particular image she or he wishes to use. Each stage involves value-judgements. It is interesting that in the same week, both *Sounds* and *NME* chose to use the same photograph of Kate Bush, using a gun to act out the lyrics of a song called 'The Man with the Golden Gun'. For most of the number she had pointed it at the audience, but the picture they chose showed it pointing upwards towards her mouth, as if simulating oral sex. Similarly, video directors make both technical *and* aesthetic choices. In the Yazoo videos,

for example, shots of singer Alison (Alf) Moyett tended to concentrate mainly on her face: big women still aren't really fashionable. Most of all, careful contrivance shapes the publicity photos that appear on hoardings, ads, and record-sleeves, as well as in the press. This manipulation reflects their unrivalled influence over the public's conception of an artist. First, women are rarely shown doing anything: Bonnie Raitt is a highly rated US slide guitarist – something you'd never guess from her record-sleeves, which are fantasy studio concoctions.

The most advanced tricks of photographic and processing technology are used in record marketing. Faces can be airbrushed, cut up, and restructured according to the judgements of the 'experts'.

Grace Jones's well-known partnership with her image-manager, Jean-Paul Goude, gave him the chance to develop his obsession with black female bodies: he depersonalized Grace Jones until she was an abstract image, an object of design – transformed into a series of geometric shapes through a technique borrowed from misogynist pop-artist Allen Jones. Effected by a kind of cosmetic surgery in the darkroom, breasts became threatening cones, buttocks and jaw-lines took on sharp edges. The resulting 'Grace Jones' was a triumph of androgynous abstraction, and a far cry from the cosy modelling shots of her that appeared in the Parisian knitting magazine, *Mon Tricot*!

A photographer who regularly works in this area explained the processes, pointing out that they are used as much on men as on women:

The difference between film and still-life is that film is like life, it's all movement and talk, but a still rests for infinity; you get to look at all the faults you wouldn't even notice in life. Retouching is an expensive 'perfecting' process and is, therefore, only considered in certain cases. For instance, when an American girl of 17, a regular cover model for *Vogue*, was photographed for a Roxy Music record-cover, the photos that came to London showed this girl with lots of pimples and red lines. So she was retouched.

If I take a picture, I'd look at it in the same way if it was a man's face, a women's face, or the label on a wine bottle. I'm looking for what's *right* in their faces. For instance, if a man's got an excess of facial hair in the wrong place, or a mole or a spot, I'd be inclined to whip it out at the retouching stage. And the same if it were a woman. It's not a question of making women more feminine, but more *perfect* in the sense of a still-life photograph. Scruffiness isn't a sales point, but perfection is.

I can see the arguments against radically changing someone's features by surgical retouching, or making someone 'sexier', but I would stand by removing people's blemishes and putting a polish on them, because I know it looks *better*.

This all sounds very reasonable. No one wants to be seen covered in blemishes. But the idea of making women 'more perfect' is in itself a value-judgement, and this is the crux of the whole issue. Who decides what a 'perfect' woman looks like if not the photographers and marketing executives? Who controls the pictures that cover girls' and women's magazines, telling us what is 'perfect' and what we should aspire to? In the majority of cases, these decisions are made by men.

The name that crops up most often in connection with successful female artists is Brian Aris. Since changing from 'page three' pictures to rock publicity shots, Aris has worked with almost all of the top female stars, including Sheena Easton, Debbie Harry, Kate Bush, Annie Lennox, Nina Hagen, and Grace Jones. As Pauline Black pointed out from her experience: 'He's all right, but he makes everyone look the same. If you're black, you come out looking whiter, if you're white, you look more WASP. Which is fine, if you want that.'

The 'look' he creates is consistent, regardless of the model. A flawless complexion, non-existent nose, dark eyes and mouth, set in stark, sculpted features with prominent cheekbones: just the way most of us wished we looked, if only in an off-guard moment of insecurity.

'Aris has a specific lighting style,' we were told. 'He uses shadowless colour photography, surrounding the person's face with a bank of light so that no shadows are shown. Not just the nose, but *anything* that sticks out (spots, for example) will be flattened. Then, using make-up and light, he brings the things out again *that he wants to show* [our emphasis].'

The appeal is seductive and, no matter how unreal, it is flattering to see such perfection – as Pauline Black found:

> He gives you cheekbones and all those things you've wished you had for years. You get the photos back and think, 'Shit, don't I look wonderful!' And then you wake up in the morning and look in the mirror and think, 'Oh, God, that's not me . . .' Basically, it's just too much to keep up.

JUMPING THROUGH THE HOOPS

'All the little hoops were set up for me to jump through, and when you jump you get a reward – an image. But it's the image *they* supply, the one that gains public approval for themselves . . . you become the Perfect Couple, or the Faded English Rose, or the Wronged Woman, or the Rock and Roll Slut, or whatever. It has very little to do with real, manageable emotions.' This was

Marianne Faithfull talking to Cynthia Rose about interviews with the press (*City Limits*, December 1981). Dolly Parton is more stoical: 'If you become a star, you make a pact with the world that you belong to them.'

The written word is a powerful tool for constructing a portrait of the artist, and a journalist needs an angle. When the writer is male, and the interviewee female, the hook is often the simplest of them all: boy meets girl.

There is little a person can do about misrepresentation. Knowing that, many bands or their managers often make up salacious little tidbits before interviews with the tabloids, to save the journalists the trouble of having to invent something themselves. It is not, for example, illegal for a writer to review a woman's body instead of her music, or for a radio DJ to salivate over a singer's looks rather than her record. It happens all the time:

> She is like some extravagantly exotic orchid ... she has a face which houses giant eyes, and pouting lips which like to smile but can just as easily make a theatrical snarl. The hair is an auburn mane. She had a small, lithe body, dancer's legs, and a suggestion of fullness of breast.

Or this:

> Grave, delicious, Kate, plump owl in her tangled nest of puzzled hair with nipples blowing tiny kisses through a cotton vest. Kate and I joined in instant photolock. Kate Bush, bushy Kate, laid out for me by the EMI artroom boys, with a gourmet's delight, like a table for guests.

Drooler number one is writing in the *Observer* (December 1978); the second is Fred Vermorel, salivating in his biography of Kate Bush.

Kate Bush is now established enough to try to fight such images, and tends to be interviewed only in trade magazines, where she discusses her experiences with and opinions of new studio technology.

We have already seen how photographic images are controlled by a consortium of photographers, marketing staff and picture editors. A similar process takes place on TV, where the impressions – and tastes – of both the camera operator and the director (almost always men) govern which shots are used. Trombonist Annie Whitehead is acutely aware of the magnetic power a woman musician has over cameramen:

> I played in a televized Christmas Party [1983] at Camden Palace, in London, and the cameramen filmed the horn section all the time. When Wham! were on TV shortly afterwards, some male friends of mine were playing in the horn section, but there wasn't a single shot of them. I *know* if I'd been there, there would have been. Cameramen on programmes like *The Tube* and *Top of the Pops* should be working for the *Sun*.

The image of Marianne Faithfull: a decadent, worldy, romantic artist; one which she herself would like the public to believe? (photo: David Corio)

CHAPTER THREE

THE MUSIC INDUSTRY IN TEN EASY LESSONS

1. THE BAND. A group of hopefuls, longing for a hit record, for fame, fortune, and *Top of the Pops*.

2. THE MANAGER. The manager's role is to 'mother' the band, to organize their day-to-day life, to negotiate work and contracts. A manager's primary function is to take care of business and finances. 'Super-managers' such as Simon Napier-Bell (Marc Bolan, Wham!), who help create their acts and often manage a whole stable of artists, still exist, as do management agencies; but more often they are simply friends who become involved. More and more women are entering this area.

3. THE A&R DEPARTMENT. Unless they want to produce their record completely independently, a band's first aim is to get a record contract. Every company has an A&R (Artists and Repertoire) department. A&R workers — most of whom are men — go out to gigs and listen to tapes that are sent in. If they like a band or artist, they will usually commission a demo-tape to be made fairly quickly in a small studio; if that turns out well, the act will be signed to the label. The A&R department is sometimes known as 'Um & Ah', due to its indecisiveness.

4. PUBLISHING. Every time a song is played on the radio or TV, or is performed by someone else, royalties are due to the writers. Their collection is dependent on the song having been published, and most record companies now have their own publishing companies. A group writing their own material may choose to set up their own company or to sign to someone else. Publishing companies spend their time looking for potential hit song writers. Like A&R, they are responsible for signing new names, and they also collect

royalties from cover versions and plays of work published by them.

5. THE STUDIO. The control-room is run by two, sometimes three, people. The *producer's* job is to direct the overall sound. Some, like Phil Spector, impose their ideas on artists who are there simply to make the basic noise he wants. Most, however, work with the artists, offering criticisms and suggestions until both sides are reasonably happy. The *engineer* makes the machinery do what the producer wants, getting the required effect out of the equipment. Increasingly, producers and engineers are working together as a permanent team, moving together from studio to studio to do different sessions, although all studios still have a resident engineer, and sometimes even a house producer. The *tape op*, or second engineer, is essentially a luxury employed by larger studios to help the engineer, set up equipment, make tea, etc. Producers, engineers and tape ops are nearly always men, as are the technicians and studio managers; studio bookings are invariably handled by women.

6. PRODUCTION, PACKING AND SALES. From the studio, the tapes are taken and made into masters, the mould from which records are pressed in the factory. A sleeve is designed and printed, the records are put inside them, and they are then packed and sent out to the shops. Dealers can phone in with orders, but chainstores such as Our Price and W.H. Smiths will negotiate huge bulk-orders of records they think will be popular. Records are also sold by reps, who go round shops trying to persuade managers to buy their product. Though the travelling reps are usually men, most of the work involved in getting a record from cutting to shop is done by women. The larger the company, the more likely it is that all the work will have been carried out by their own staff: smaller companies will employ outside agencies or pay multinationals such as EMI to press, pack, distribute or market their records.

7. PROMOTION. When the record is released, the priority is to get it played on the radio. This is the job of the promotions department, whose 'pluggers' try to persuade radio-show producers and DJs to give their songs airplay (by taking them out to dinner, for instance). This department also ensures that record shops have advertising posters and display their records, and that the shops are provided with tour programmes and other promotional material. The artist and/or their publishing company may also decide to employ independent pluggers to push certain records.

8. PRESS. Meanwhile, the press department is working hard to get our budding stars splashed all over the media. They liaise with the media, commission photo-sessions for publicity shots, try to get records and gigs reviewed, send out press releases to tell everyone what artists are doing, dream up gimmicks, 'leak' gossip, and approach editors with ideas for stories. Most of this work is done by women and within the record company, although some people prefer to hire their own publicists/agencies.

9. TOURING. In general, the bigger the show, the bigger the entourage. Any tour will usually have roadies to move and set up equipment, lighting crews, sound crews, and an engineer to mix the sound live. This area, again, is almost exclusively male.

10. DJs AND JOURNALISTS. These play an essential part in getting a record across to potential customers!

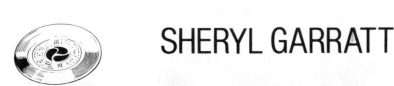

SHERYL GARRATT

Women at EMI's distribution plant packing copies of an album for the press, 1983. (photo: Hetti Church)

WORKING 9 TO 5

The record business. Glamour and Big Money. Late-night clubs and famous faces. Being part of it, involved in the bustle behind the scenes: soundchecks, interviews, all-night recording sessions, exotic places, sex, drugs, the high life. Arranging the lights, mixing the sound, taking the photos, hustling the heroes past screaming fans into the waiting car . . . Just *being there*, being in the know. Because the music business is exciting and important. It is high-speed, 24-hour fun. It is an alternative to mundane routine. Sweet dreams are made of this . . .

The reality is very different. One of the engineers at EMI's hallowed Abbey Road Studios, London, said he'd seen more drugs and wild parties, more *genuine* good times, in his old job in a factory than he'd ever experienced with the musicians he now works with. Most of the work involved in the industry is boring, menial and – apart from the odd glimpse of a passing superstar, perhaps – totally unglamorous. The myth persists because being a pop star is one of the few escapes open to most working-class kids, it fills adolescent daydreams, and we long to be that man or woman at the concert who's got a backstage pass. It persists, most of all, because the people in the industry *want* it to, because it is in their interests to perpetuate it. Stardust attracts, and many of the women interviewed in this chapter started in the industry as fans. No one is impressed if you type memos or book hotels for a living . . . but if the memo concerns Barry Manilow? Or the hotel room is for Duran Duran? Women, especially, tend to be judged by the status of the men they associate with and, even if they never meet them, at least they're dealing with Those Names.

The rock business is still a boy's game. Even now, very few women get into positions of *real* power where they have direct influence on the look or the sound of the finished product. For most, the novelty of Famous Faces wears off and it's just a job like any other. For many, it was never anything else. 'Every time I hear a record, I automatically repeat the catalogue number. Music is just a series of numbers to me now' (sales telephonist, EMI).

This is the invisible, decidedly unglamorous side of the industry, the places where many of the 'women in rock' work. Most of the major labels – and, indirectly, the independents – probably employ as many women as men, perhaps even more: 'tea ladies', secretaries, receptionists, canteen staff, cleaners, and almost anyone servicing the needs of the people within the industry will be female. Women also do all of the menial work that cannot yet be done more cheaply by machines: they assemble the basic parts of instruments, solder the wires and chips of electrical equipment and, in the pressing and packing plants, it is women who check the quality of discs, put them in their sleeves and pack shop orders into boxes ready for distribution. They are the anonymous factory-workers at the bottom of the company hierarchy, and almost every record is handled by them at some point. Which gives them, if they choose to use it, an enormous amount of power.

The following gem is a Virgin Records press release from late 1973:

The formidable ladies of EMI's packaging department appear to exercise a degree of censorship far stricter than any of the company's own producers or executives would contemplate. Album-sleeves they don't like, for example, they won't pack. Latest victim of the country's most solicitous assembly-line is the sleeve of *Angel's Egg*, the new Gong album . . . The front cover's idyllic village scene features a floating quim [in fact, a cartoon of a naked woman on her back with her legs open] in the top right-hand corner. Said quim, together with the legend 'Motha Fucker' on the back of the sleeve did the trick. The ladies downed tools and packed up, so to speak. I personally am in favour of anyone on any assembly-line refusing to do anything, no matter how trivial or petty!

Yes, indeed, boys.

When questioned by *Spare Rib* at the time, Virgin claimed that 'It was a joke – we really suffer because of them.' And the problem seems to have continued, both for Virgin (remember the fuss over the Sex Pistols' *Never Mind the Bollocks* sleeve?), and for other companies. Designers often have to take the feelings of these workers into account if they want to be sure that the record – and sleeve – will reach the shops on time.

EMI's plant in Middlesex is, in fact, reputed to be one of the better factories: it is unionized, working conditions are fair, and the company was happy to let me visit. The manager, Kerry Humphries, is a large, middle-aged, genial man who calls his staff 'girls' (some of them are grandmothers), and thinks his secretary is wonderful. He forgot to mention her name: he calls her 'Darling'. He meant well.

When I asked about disputes at the factory, Humphries immediately assumed I meant the Pistols: EMI became the first label to drop the band, partly due to pressure from workers who objected to packing the 'Anarchy in the UK' single.

> It was a very emotive situation, very disheartening, too, because we lost a good act as far as I was concerned. I think we've bitterly regretted it ever since, and I think the people on the floor regretted it as well. It was a moral thing, led by a nucleus of people who objected, and it gained momentum. Then we lost them, and they were a very big success, as you know. Now

Cheaper than machines: EMI forty years earlier.
(photo: courtesy EMI Records)

we don't care, if people want to buy it – it's only if it's *really* objectionable that perhaps we don't close our eyes to it. To survive, you have to run with them rather than against them, and people are now sensitive to there being greater things outside to object to – porno shops and things like that. It's up to the retailer to use discretion, in records as in anything else. To the people that handle it, I think it's just another object, like picking up an ashtray. They just accept it.

But why are so many of the 'people' handling records at the plant women? 'I find women more productive than the men, because they're more responsive, they're more sensitive creatures ...' Outside his office the telephone sales staff sit at VDUs: they take telephone orders from dealers and type them into their machines. Humphries calls them, 'our front line troops'. Including bulk orders from the chainstores, as much as 75 per cent of the total sales of a record can be sold from the office in this way, according to Virgin's former sales manager, Ann Kelly. The remaining sales are made by the (male) travelling reps.

Kelly explained why, when she first set up Virgin's own sales-force, she employed a totally male staff:

Obviously, being a woman I'm not chauvinist in any way, but there were very few women who came to the interviews. The ones that did come had a total lack of experience, and at the time we needed that. The areas they had to cover were huge, and it was pretty weird material at the time. It's much more mainstream at the moment, but then Virgin had Henry Cow, Egg, Slapp Happy ... And my experience of women 'on the road' is that they would rather be at home. I don't mean they don't do the work, but a lot of women are married, and anybody who wants to get on, they don't really want to be a rep, they would rather be in the office.

Women's home responsibilities, lack of relevant experience, and the fact that they just don't apply for certain jobs were the recurrent reasons given for their absence from various areas – usually, the better-paid jobs. Ann Kelly admits that she herself was able to combine work and family with little difficulty. But for the time being, it seems that women will remain at the office typewriter while the reps get the company cars (although their job is hardly glamorous or easy).

At EMI, telephone orders go straight into a computer. On the floor below, where the orders are fed out, women collect the records required in trolleys and pack them into boxes. The only man around when I visited was Cyril, there for the heavy lifting-work. As the supervisor put it, 'The majority of us have done enough work for one lifetime, lifting shopping and babies and all.' Cyril flirted a little: 'If there was more like you here, I'd work overtime ...' The women, however, were quick to respond, and he wilted visibly as the jokes got increasingly raucous. The single being packed ready for release that week was Queen's 'Body Language', packaged in a picture bag that showed a woman lying with her head on a man's belly, her mouth slightly open. Arrows on her naked body pointed to him, on his body they pointed down. Subtle, that. What did they think about it? 'I haven't really looked. What is it?' 'Which way way round does it go?' 'Oooh, I think it's rude!' Then a more thoughtful, 'But it's so unnecessary. Groups like Queen would sell if they put it in brown paper bags. Why do they do it?'

And would they still refuse to handle anything they found offensive?

'Well, we stopped those punk people didn't we?

What were they? The Sex Pistols.'

Nods of agreement all along, laughs of triumph. Mr Humphries's girls aren't so sorry after all.

Sadly, all of them were shocked at any suggestion that they use their power for more 'selfish' reasons – more money, for instance. Shortly after my visit, the workforce was cut and job losses accepted with very little opposition. The general feeling seemed to be gratitude to the company for offering such short, convenient hours (most were working on four-hour shifts), and all were quick to point out that there was no other way they *could* work. Employers are equally quick to exploit this, of course: female labour is more than just 'responsive'. It's cheap, too.

Why *are* there no men, I ask.

'It's not a man's work, really, is it? The majority of men don't want to work part-time.'

'They haven't got the intelligence, have they?' joked Ruby, while Pat offered the notion that 'It's always been that way. The women do all the graft, and the men do the bits and bobs.'

The EMI plant is in no way unique in its use of female labour. If anything, conditions for the women workers there are above average, given that this plant's efficient union representation and organization are rare in the industry. Jane Hutch worked for Soundcraft, one of the top companies designing and building mixing-decks in Britain. She describes a factory set-up very similar to EMI:

I probably had the most interesting job on the technical side, testing mixers. But generally, women did the mindless work like soldering – you're not given a lot of encouragement to move up. Married women make good employees, because they don't really want more responsibility at work. They've got enough at home looking after a husband and kids, paying the bills, and thinking about what to have for tea and stuff. They want a job you can do while you're listening to the radio, where you don't really have to worry. It's mainly young, single women, I suppose, who want something out of work.'

IN A MAN'S WORLD

When I started DinDisc [a subsidiary label of Virgin], people said that they didn't think it would work with me running a record company, because they didn't think that men would work for me. They seemed to think it was essential to *have* men in a company. And then they said that they didn't think groups would sign to a woman. This was in 1979. I had signed the Human League, Buzzcocks, J.J.Cale, Tom Petty and the Police, and they said that!

— Carol Wilson, Director of the independent record company InterDisc

Even if women do want to work in higher-status jobs, there are still obstacles – the main one being good, old-fashioned prejudice. The antiquated attitudes of male chauvinism still exist, but nowadays they're more subtle and insidious. It's harder to pin down, impossible to prove – often even unintentional – and it is easy for the victim to blame herself or to doubt her abilities because of it. As journalist Caroline Coon remarked:

You can't believe they're being so trivial. I always thought I was a 'he', a 'mankind', I thought I was included, and it was a great shock to plunge into the real world and to realize that I wasn't. But at first, one doesn't take it personally. One is too well-mannered and unparanoid to think that all that game-playing is anything to do with gender. It must be about your *writing*. When you do finally cotton on, it's a relief, but also a great disappointment. It's intimidation.

That's what they're doing it for – it's the closed-shop syndrome.

The theme recurs continually in interviews. From women who were vehemently anti-feminist; from women in all positions in all areas of the industry; and from women who had nothing in common except their gender and their shared experience of the music industry. Sometimes I had the feeling that I was listening to the same words again and again: only the voices were different. Julie Burchill, journalist and one-time NME staff writer:

> Me and Tony [Parsons, – her husband] got asked out to lunch by Moira Bellas, who was head of press at Warners, and the other staff at NME said, 'Oh, God, she's an old dragon! She really puts the men at Warner Brothers through hell, bossing them about!' Because she had a bit of power, they obviously didn't like her at all. We were prepared to meet this old monster with a bull-whip, but she was lovely! She'd been a mod, been on *Ready Steady Go!* and everything, and she had some really great stories. But they like their press officers to be girlish and giggly, making insinuations all the time about their virility, and they didn't like Moira because she didn't do any of that.'

Apart from the secretaries who do a large part of the work in all departments in the big, happy record-company family, a woman's place is in the press department. Vivien Goldman was press officer for Island Records at the time of Bob Marley and the Wailers' breakthrough concert at the Lyceum:

> I pushed and pushed until I got them on front covers everywhere – that was really my peak as a PR, because I loved them so much. After that, I swore I'd never go back

into publicity because it's so frustrating a job – you're so dependent on other people whims. A really big PR can bargain, 'Yes, will give you an interview with this big star, but only if you run such and such as well.' But unless you've got that sort of blackmail power, you've got none at all. The quality of your acts comes into it a lot, but otherwise all you've got going for you is your charm. That's why women aren't allowed out of the press ghetto. You've got to take the mostly male journalists out to lunch, and be so nice that when you phone them up with suggestions, they're going to want to talk to you. It's like a hooker thing, you have to please and try to elicit the desired response. But it's never in your control whether it's going to go well or not.

Another journalist, Penny Valentine, also has few pleasant memories of her time as a press officer:

> You had to 'nanny' people, you had to make sure everyone was comfortable, to make sure they all had drinks at receptions, that they had everything they wanted. And if they phoned up wingeing about how to get there, you'd run a car. It was just like running a bloody kindergarten, except that the people you were dealing with weren't as nice as kids. It was a total service job.

On the other side, Arista's head of press, Versa Manos, explained that she has considerable power in her job, and that in most companies press people are consulted about issues such as the design of sleeves and posters, and the image of their acts. Their views are listened to and acted upon.

But A&R is still the department that determines the profile of the company, what its acts actually *sound* like. Brian Southall, EMI's spokesperson, ained women's ghettoization in press jobs their almost complete non-representation in . thus: 'I don't think they'd like A&R. It olves very odd hours, and going out alone at ree in the morning to listen to weird music in eird clubs just wouldn't be nice, would it?' rejudice veiled as paternalism: as a journalist ind as a fan, I've been doing just that for years, and it's odd how such companies have no qualms about sending me out, all on my own, to do interviews in places I don't know, or to spend the night in strange hotels . . . Perhaps the real answer is that boys just don't want girls spoiling their party, as this story from Ann Kelly suggests:

Sales managers and directors from all the companies used to get together every six months to talk about the industry. Christmas was coming up, probably in my second year as sales manager, and at the previous meeting they had discussed it and set a date. But the organizer had changed the date and the venue, and didn't tell me – a certain group of them had chatted and decided 'Ann'll not want to come.' They basically wanted a good night out with the boys. It wouldn't have bothered me, quite honestly, if they'd have come out and said that. But I was talking to someone at CBS and he mentioned it accidentally – I was, of course, very annoyed and phoned up the guy. In fact, Brian Mulligan, who then ran *Record Business*, put a bit in his column saying, 'Is Ann Kelly giving the industry chauvinist ties for Christmas?' Of course, I didn't! But the following year, they made sure I'd been invited.

Promotion is another prickly subject. One of the women interviewed told how she was once asked to train her new boss: 'They took on a bloke to run production, and they asked me to train him so that eventually he would have been

paid more. I had a big row, but in the end we got paid the same money. And I had to train him.' A similar problem recurs with the secretary who does her boss's job for years, only to see him eventually replaced with another man, whom she's expected to help. Even in the predominantly female press offices, the head of department will often be a man.

Carol Wilson set up and ran Virgin Records' publishing company, Virgin Music, eventually signing groups like the Police and the Buzzcocks. At first she found the attitudes of men a serious problem:

For the first three years, almost every time I walked into a man's office, I would get humiliated in some way or another. I remember taking a song to someone who's quite well known in the business, and he said, 'Which one of the writers are you sleeping with?' I never walked out when I got these insults because if I had, I would've lost contact after contact. People can accept the *idea* of a woman in business, maybe, but they expect her to be tall and big-boned and commanding. When they meet someone who's little and blonde and has a turned-up nose, they don't take you seriously. I went through a phase when I cut off my hair, stopped wearing make-up, and wore very plain, totally unfeminine clothes – anoraks and things – because I felt people took me more seriously when I looked like that. It wasn't until the last couple of years that I softened up again because now I've got a track record to roll out.

Carol now runs her own, independent record label, Interdisc.

In spite of this kind of story, almost every woman we spoke to for this chapter mentioned other women: slowly, quietly, progress is being made. Jill Sinclair is one of the three directors of

Sylvia Robinson, Queen of Sugarhill, at work in her office at the label's New Jersey studios. The gold discs on the walls are all records produced by her. (photo: Val Wilmer/Format)

the ZTT (of Frankie Goes to Hollywood fame). In the US, Suzanne de Passe is vice-president of Motown (she was responsible for signing groups like the Commodores to the label), and Noreen Woods and Bunny Freidus are vice-presidents of Alantic and CBS respectively. In Jamaica, Rita Marley helped to build the impressive Tuff Gong set-up from the Wailin' Souls record 'shack' which she opened with Bob in 1966; since her husband's death, she has run the operation alone. As well as the label and publishing company, the independent outfit presses its own records, distributes them, and owns a popular 24-track studio.

Surprisingly, though, the much-trumpeted rise of the independent labels in the 1970s didn't offer new opportunities to women. The new companies usually followed the same sexist structures laid down by the majors they sought to subvert.

Black music, however, has always had to rely on small labels for its survival, and here many more women are involved. British lovers'-rock singers such as Carroll Thompson and Jean Adebambo run their own labels. On the Jamaican reggae scene, Judy Mowatt has the Ashandan label, while Sonia Pottinger has owned several companies, including the respected Tip Top, Sky Note, and High Note labels. In the USA, producer Sylvia Robinson and her husband Joe own the Sugarhill/All-Platinum empire, famed for its rap artists and for its recent acquisition of historic records on the Chess/Checker/Cadet labels. Unable to get a suitable deal from an established company, singer Betty Carter is one of the many jazz artists to found her own label, Bet-Car.

Also in the US, there is the 'women's music' industry, a music with a strong lesbian consciousness that grew out of the women's movement of the early 1970s. Unlike Britain, where feminist labels such as Stroppy Cow are still tiny and relatively insignificant, the US labels gross two million dollars and sell around 200,000 records per year. There are separate 'Women's Music' sections in most shops, and the market for this often fairly safe, folksy-sounding music, is growing. The first label to declare itself a 'national women's recording company' was Olivia, which began with a tour by Meg Christian, now one of the genre's biggest stars. The US magazine *Mother Jones* tells the story:

> After Christian performed, Berson [Ginny Berson, founder, now head of women's programming on a California radio station] would give a rap about how Olivia needed distributors for its records. The woman who raised her hand became the town's Olivia distributor. Before long, there were 40 distributors – now winnowed down to a less unwieldy 15 – who began carrying not just Olivia records but any women's music recordings. In starting a record company, Olivia actually organized an industry.

Money for new releases is found by raising small loans from women across the country, the Washington-based agency Roadwork organizes bookings for many of the artists, and there are regular national Women's Music festivals. Redwood and Pleiades are also run by women for women – although, as the companies get larger and more concerned with commercial success, more men appear to be getting involved. As yet, there just aren't enough women with the necessary experience and contacts to service such an expanding industry.

Separatism was never as strong a practice in Britain as in the USA. WRPM(Women's Revolutions Per Minute) distribute women's music in the UK, and have organized national distribution. But the tendency is for women to work within established companies. The *Making Waves* album on the Girlfriend label, for example, was produced by women to showcase women's bands, offered a rich and varied range of music, and was distributed by Rough Trade. Women are finding ways to release their music on their own terms.

But in the end, does it really matter who is in charge? Does it really matter whether the boss is male or female? I've worked for women, and apart from a little more understanding and a lot less groping and boring innuendo, there wasn't much difference. Dealing with Carol Wilson at InterDisc made it easier for manager Christine Robertson to take her child into the company office. Top PR Alison Short says she wouldn't dream of calling her assistant a secretary. Others claim they make a positive effort to encourage women in their departments.

On the whole, though, they are working under the same pressure, to the same rules, and in the same society as a man. Their job is to make profits, and if they fail, they will eventually lose their job. And they are being watched closely, much more closely than a man in the same position would be – they have to prove themselves. It's the whole game, not a few rules, that really needs changing.

BACKSTAGE PASSES

It was the first political group I'd been involved in apart from at college, and I was pretty inexperienced. I never used to say much in meetings at all, deciding about gigs and policy and so on. But when the editorial collective was set up for the magazine [*Temporary Hoarding*], I felt more confident there. I was able to write about sexual politics, and to get those ideas across to a new audience in an accessible way. I think now that the way Rock Against Racism (RAR) worked was actually quite oppressive to the women involved, but I was too inexperienced to work out what was going on. You could be involved in all that in 1977, 1978: being really avid about the news and all the stuff leading up to the 1979 election, all the marches against the National Front and everything. It was frightening, but also very exciting to be involved in it all. It was great fun.

Member of London Rock Against Racism Lucy Whitman (née Toothpaste) here sums up the whole do-it-yourself attitude that was encouraged by punk and flourished with the start of Rock Against Racism. RAR taught me a lot about politics, but even more about music. Its leaflets always had a point-by-point guide to organizing a gig, from booking the PA to printing up posters. The national office, run by 'Irate' Kate Webb, had a list of contacts for bands, but you usually didn't have to look that far: groups were springing up everywhere and clamouring for gigs. For the more established local bands, it meant a chance to be seen outside their home area, and, like the Au Pairs, many came to national attention through the RAR/RAS(Rock Against Sexism) circuit. 'It was the way we started getting known in London,' recalls former Au Pairs singer Lesley Woods, herself a member of the Birmingham RAR

group. 'But also it was a really important cultural thing at that time, a big organization with branches all over the country. It was all part of a period when you look back on it – really lively, really good energy, anarchic. It was brilliant. Ah, nostalgia!'

Totally inexperienced people were running clubs, arranging national tours, organizing gigs – not just for RAR, but for any other cause that could rally a few bands to support them. Anyone could do it, and many of those involved were women. For the first time, the mysteries of stage management were revealed to all. RAS, obviously, gave even more women the chance to learn. Lucy Whitman vividly remembers organizing one of RAS's first major gigs – the Spoilsports, Delta 5, and the Gang of Four at London's Electric Ballroom: 'I'm astounded, now, at what I did. It all seemed so easy then.'

In retrospect, there were faults in both RAR and RAS, but at the time it felt totally right. Whatever effect they had politically (and RAR and the Anti-Nazi League *did* play a part in the NF's 1979 defeat), they gave a lot of women the chance to play in a more supportive environment. Both organizations were instrumental in demystifying the skills needed to promote live music – and many of us are still using the knowledge. Rock Against Racism and its numerous offspring thus changed the alternative-gig circuit irrevocably. The same cannot be said of commercial concert promotion, where men still dominate the road, sound and lighting crews who handle heavy lifting and the technical side. Perhaps the persistent image of life 'on the road' helps maintain their monopoly. The reality is different, of course: anyone who has sat through the tedium of a sound check, or watched a rig being dismantled late at night, will know that a roadie's job is hardly exciting – if anything the all-lads-together camaraderie probably helps while away boredom! The atmosphere *is* intimidating, and female musicians often talked of the loneliness they felt on tour. Alannah Currie of the Thompson Twins spoke of her relief at having another woman, keyboard-player Carrie Booth, on their recent tours; Pauline Black spoke with gratitude of her manager, Juliet Devie. When singing with Culture Club, Helen Terry too found problems:

> The first tour I did with them, I hung out with the road crew, just generally being one of the boys. I came back with the most appalling language and habits, and I was ill for two weeks afterwards, dead sick. So I realized that I'd rather be by myself and feel lonely than ruin my health; on tour now, I keep myself very much to myself. I love being on stage, but I hate the travelling, the waiting, the boredom.

Even in this area, though, there are a handful of women. Jane Spiers began as a lighting technician in a theatre in New Zealand, but decided she enjoyed working for visiting rock bands more. Since then, she has arranged lighting for names such as the Selecter, Imagination, the Police, Peter Tosh, and Depeche Mode. She claims that the stereotype of the neanderthal, macho-man roadie is now way off the mark: 'There's still a few of those around, but mainly they're just doing a job and trying to earn money for their families, just like anyone else. It's a lot more professional now.'

Christine Robertson, who was part of the management of the Slits and the Pop Group, did the lights on their tours. During one show in Florence she literally came to blows when she was told by the male technician that she couldn't touch the operating-board. 'It was very funny. All I wanted to do was to work the lights.' Generally, though, she doesn't see her gender as a problem in her particular job:

Companies will take notice of what you say as a manager because they *have* to – they've made an investment in a group and they've got to protect that, so they won't talk down to a manager in the same way as they would an employee. I think it's a lot to do with personality, as well – when I met those sort of patronizing attitudes, I probably laughed or gave them back as good as they gave me. I mean, a man may say [pompous voice], 'Oh, you're only a woman, you can't do these things.' But I'd just say, 'So what, you're only a bloody man!'

Vicki Wickham, who produced and managed LaBelle, and now works for Nona Hendryx, amongst others, has a similar attitude:

> I enjoy what I do and I do it, and it's not in my head that anyone would ever say that you're a woman and you can't. I walk into an auditorium when we're setting up, and I know what I want done, and I know how to get it. I never think that this union crew of 25 older guys must be thinking, 'Who is this weird bird?' until somebody sometimes will laugh about it. There are more women managers now, too, which is very encouraging, so I feel I'm not alone in that.

Before the late 1970s, women like Suzy Watson-Taylor (manager of the Incredible String Band) or Eve Taylor (who worked for Sandie Shaw and Adam Faith) were exceptional in pop. Even after punk supposedly opened the floodgates, the fact that a band in the league of the Only Ones should have a female manager attracted attention. But now, many of the managers I speak to are women, and even if the name I am given to contact is male, the work seems to be carried out completely by female 'assistants'.

None the less, women are still not totally acceptable, as Christine Robertson discovered when she continued to work during and after her pregnancy:

I went to a record company meeting with a man I knew quite well, in the business sense. It was quite an important meeting which I didn't want to miss, but my labour pains had already started, and I had to rush to hospital straight after it. When I told him later, he said to the group, 'She can't go on managing you, she's going to need to be a mother for the next few years.' And to me, 'You'll find you won't be able to do anything if you have a child.' Children *are* a distrac-

tion when they're young, but I think it makes you fitter, actually, it sharpens you up. It's not a problem.

Caroline Coon found similar problems with her femininity when she stepped in to manage the Clash after their split with Bernie Rhodes:

It was one of the few times in my life when I honestly wished I was a man, when I felt my physical experience coming between me and what was going on. The Clash would have been much happier if I was male, and, essentially, I was there to make them happy. I wanted to keep them on the road.

Barbara Jeffries, manager of the Townhouse Studios, London.

But whatever I did was sabotaged by the fact that I had tits. It worked itself out – they found men who they thought could do the job for them. Actually, they were very fair in the circumstances, and it was one of the most exciting nine months of my life. But my feelings for the record company [CBS] are a different thing altogether... the look on their faces when I walked in as the band's temporary organizer was a sight to be believed! But you have to overlook sexism, you really do. It *is* possible for women to do it. It's physically possible, it's mentally possible. What you've got to do is know what you're up against – then overcome it and forget it. There's plenty of time behind closed doors to get angry; on the job, your actions are proof of their slander.

Vicki Wickham doesn't feel that things have improved that substantially in her 10 years in the business:

The only thing is, thank heavens, that women have got smarter. And I don't think the biz itself looks on women as quite such idiots as it used to – they still don't like us, but they've learned that they have to suffer it, that some of us are going to be around whether they like it or not.

BEHIND THE MIXING-DESK

I don't think women are made aware of professions like this. When I was at school, I remember a careers class where they asked what we wanted to do, and one girl actually said, 'I want to be a sound technician in a studio.' And everyone gasped and said, 'A what...?' All the others had said a hairdresser and a secretary and things. It was a total shock.

    — Karin Clayton, former tape op,
now manager of the SARM Studios

Women Live: Viv Acious is a sound engineer for several London-based women's bands. She also runs workshops to teach her skills. (photo: Jane Ralley)

Girls don't work in studios. There have been a handful of women producers, but certainly no Phil Spector or Lee Perry – no one who has created a recognizable 'sound' or pioneered new directions. The reasons are pretty clear, and go right back to Janet and John books, where the little girl helps mother in the kitchen while the boy goes toddling off to watch daddy mend the car. Girls aren't encouraged or taught to use tools and machines (apart from household appliances, of course). At school they learn cookery and needlework instead of woodwork or metalwork; they are channelled into the arts rather than the sciences. I was 20 years old before I even learned to fit a plug by which time learning such a simple task was incredibly hard, because I'd been conditioned into a disease that tends to affect women in our society: technophobia, fear of knobs and wires. It's crippling.

'Very, very few girls apply,' said Barbara Jeffries, manager of the Townhouse Studios in London:

In the 12 years I've been working in studios, there's only been one girl who passed an interview. Usually, their understanding of what they're applying for is wrong. It sounds really derogatory, but they've no conception that they're going to have to come in and work 15 hours a day, or learn something in the evening and be able to apply it the next day. Which you have to here, because it's such a quick industry. The boys are actually better equipped when they come for a job because they've read up, they've thought about it. They don't just read the music press, they read the technical press, and they've got a bit of insight into what the job entails.

Music is sold in girls' magazines on image and on lyrics: there are rarely pictures of bands even playing, let alone discussing their ideas or technique. Young women are largely excluded from the groups who go home together after school to play on guitars, to mess around with tapes and to take things apart. 'You just can't see a group of girls going home with a soldering iron,' noted Barbara. 'And that's another question we ask – if they know how to use one. You want to know if they've got that sort of equipment and if they've linked this to that, and, invariably, the boys have. They get an earlier interest, and they follow it through.'

But let's just suppose that somehow a woman *did* develop these interests, had learned to play and to use simple technology, and had been interested in Culture Club because of Steve Levine's production or Jon Moss's drumming rather than Boy George's style (in spite of the way *Jackie* had presented them). She decides that she wants to work in the studio. Mysteriously, she'll find that many of her applications get no reply. 'We make a point of seeing girls,' stated Barbara, 'but I think a lot of people don't even bother.'

Obviously, I haven't found a studio willing to

admit that they operate a men-only policy. Many, however, felt that having a woman around would cause problems at times. 'There are certain sessions where women just wouldn't be able to work,' declared one engineer firmly – the implication being that some male musicians would spend so much time hassling a woman that expensive studio time would be lost, or she just wouldn't be able to do her job.

Records are no longer made live in one take, an album in a fortnight. It can take well over a month to make just a single . . . a month of listening to the same guitar riff a hundred times, of hearing each syllable of each word in the lyrics again and again. The hours can be long and unsociable: to spend 15 hours at a stretch in the studio for weeks on end is not unusual. Barbara Jeffries:

> If you're all girls together you tend to be a lot looser in your discussions and conversations than if there was a man around. And the same when there's a lot of men together, they want to horseplay around. And you *must*, really, if you're in there so long.

In most studios, there is a general air of all-lads-together camaraderie. Even the equipment colludes: if a wrong instruction is fed into a Solid State Logic computer desk, it won't give a simple 'error' message. Instead, the screen flashes increasingly coarse abuse. 'These are genuine insults,' crows the SL 4000 E mixer manual, 'If you don't like them, don't use them.' It may sound petty or puritanical to complain about a machine being programmed to say, 'Go screw yourself with a poker' (and that's one of the softer insults). But this is the latest in studio technology, and the fact that it was added tells us a lot about the attitudes of its makers and users.

Back to our heroine, though. She has now overcome all obstacles and has become a good tape op: a fairly simple job where personality is as important as technical skill, anyway. Barbara Jeffries again:

> We did have one girl who we employed for four years, and she was a brilliant tape op, and would have been a great engineer. But in the end, she didn't have the confidence. We'd all keep saying, 'But you could do this session, you really could do it very well.' Then on the day, she'd just collapse in nerves and not be able to do it. I'm not saying *all* women would act that way, but because a girl on the recording side is very rare, there's more pressure on you to be above and beyond the men. If any small thing goes wrong, it's blamed on her being a girl, that she's not really up to the mark.

The studio atmosphere can also be inhibiting to women artists, who are often victims of the dreaded technophobia, and less confident about asking questions or demanding what they want. Pressures of time, possessiveness about their skills, or even sheer laziness can make engineers and producers unwilling to explain what they are doing, or what can or cannot be done. They may even ignore women's ideas completely, imagining themselves some sort of Svengali figure – the ghost of Phil Spector lingers on long after his (creative) death.

Hazel O'Connor described how her early producers rarely consulted her about how she wanted her songs to sound. When working with Tony Visconti on *Breaking Glass*, she was amazed when he asked her to play her tunes first to show him how they should feel: 'Before, I'd have to sit there watching people play my stuff, and everything was totally out of my control. You're always really afraid you're going to put your foot in it, or that somebody's going to drop you like a hot brick if you say what you think would be right.'

The Belle Stars talked of similar problems with producer Peter Collins, who was unwilling to let them play their parts unless they could work to his standards. They expressed their relief at working with a woman, Ann Dudley. Out of the album's worth of material they recorded with her, however, only one single, 'The Entertainer', has so far been released, and the band are now back with Collins. For the Raincoats, the problem was not lack of faith in their musical abilities, however, but political differences. Vicki Aspinall:

> When we recorded 'Animal Rhapsody', which is a song about women's sexuality, Gina flunked out of it three times because of a male engineer. He took exception to the words, started to make remarks about them, and seemed to be quite threatened, I think. And she found it rather off-putting. Especially when you're recording a vocal, you feel exposed to the engineer: he can hear every word. She would have felt more comfortable with a woman. It was quite funny, actually, to watch his reactions; but we were aware of him as a stage between us and the music.

A simple solution, of course, is for women to produce themselves. In 1981 lovers'-rock singer Carroll Thompson set up her own company, C&B, and began to produce her own material because

> We had so much hassle to get what we wanted that we thought we might as well do it ourselves. Louisa Mark, Brown Sugar, Janet Kay and 15, 16, & 17 were the only women having any success, and I don't think the producers took us seriously. They thought, 'Oh, they'll just get pregnant and give up, or their man will give them a whole heap of trouble, and there's no point putting money into it.' After a while it changed as they realized that women weren't stupid, that

they *did* want to make a career out of singing. For me, producing was a natural step because when you write a song, you know how you want it. I'm lucky in that I have some good, patient musicians who are willing to try it all ways until we get danceability and listening power. That's what it's all about. It's easy, really. If you go to a party and can see what everyone else likes, it's not too hard to come back and emulate it.

Another woman who began by producing herself was soul singer Sylvia Robinson, now better known as the woman who brought rapping to the world's attention with the Sugarhill Gang's 'Rapper's Delight'. She produced hits such as Grandmaster Flash and the Furious Five's 'The Message' in two studios in New Jersey, releasing them on Sugarhill, the label she owns along with her husband, Joe. Son Joey is one of the company's 40-odd workers, and also a member of one of their less successful bands, West St Mob. The other children call into the Sugarhill buildings after school, and the whole company seems to revolve around her. 'This being my own business, I don't really have any problems,' she smiled.

I don't really know any other women producers, because my whole life is here between the studios, home, and my kids, so I don't get to see what's going on in the outside world. I'd like to see other women involved because it's so nice, that freedom to express. I love it! I find that producing them, I feel like it's *me*. Usually, artists have a certain amount of ego, but in producing you get the same feeling, and if it's a hit, you feel like you did it. It's very gratifying, and anything men can do, women can do better!

Sylvia is obviously a lady who is happy in her job,

as she purrs in one of her now-rare releases as a vocalist ('It's Good to be the Queen'):

I rule the land of Rappersville
A castle on the hill called Sugarhill
Like Diana Ross I'm loud and clear
This is my house, I live here . . .
I consider myself a fortunate lady
Sporting my Rolls and my grey Mercedes.

Not everyone is as happy, though: in 1984 Grandmaster Flash won a court battle against the Queen, retaining the rights to his name and forcing her to open Sugarhill's accounts and pay him his correct royalties.

The traditional route from tape op to engineer has so far been successfully negotiated by only a handful of women – Corinne Simcock manages John Foxx's 24-track studio in London as well as engineering there, and Melanie West, at Sigma Sound in New York, is also highly rated. But most women still come to production as performers. Kate Bush, Joni Mitchell, Carole King, Patrice Rushen and Millie Jackson are just a few of the many women who today produce their own material, while Thérèse Bazar began producing others after the break-up of her own pop duo, Dollar. New York electro-funk producer Lotti Golden (WARP-9, Chilltown) began her career as a songwriter and singer at the tender age of 14. Her experience as a vocalist has helped her to direct the women singers she sometimes produces:

I was fascinated with the studio. Live performing was OK, but the handicaps of bad sound systems and loud guitar-players were difficult realities for me. The studio was where I loved to create: in that wonderful world of sound, anything was possible. Most producers haven't been formally trained in studio technology, unless they were recording engineers first,

Lotti Golden, New York record producer, at work.   (photo: Patricia Bates)

like many rock producers. For me, it has been learning on the job. You pick up something from every engineer you work with. You ask questions, and you learn from being in the environment. I've been producing for two years now, working with a co-producer, Richard Scher. Because Richard is a man, I might have been more privy to the world of production, but it's hard to say. When we were mixing WARP-9's 'No Man Is An Island', we ran into Sergio Munzaibai and John Morales, a production/mixing team we'd never met before, even though we knew and respected each other's work. The rapport was immediate: exchanging ideas, studio and record talk. I never get the feeling from my peers that I'm not on par because I'm a woman. It's a professional environment, and it's the quality of your work that counts. The male engineers and musicians that I work with have been great, although a while back I did find in business meetings with record executives and A&R people, that many of them assumed that Richard and I were either married or going out. I hope this is the last vestige in the music business of 'How can a lady be here on her own merit?'

British producer Ann Dudley, who now works mainly at the SARM Studios and as part of the ZTT/Art of Noise conglomerate, came in by another route. Classically trained at the Royal College of Music, she also worked in bands and as a session keyboard-player, meeting Trevor Horn just as he was starting as a producer. Her musical knowledge, as well as her understanding of pop, put her in great demand as an arranger, and when Horn became successful, they began to work together with names such as Dollar, ABC, Spandau Ballet and Malcolm McLaren. From arranger and musician to producer seemed a logical step, and she feels that a good ear is as important as any great technical skill: 'It all boils down to being able to hear things that aren't there. If you can't do that, you'll never be a good record producer. You've got to be able to listen to a demo that might be appalling – somebody sitting at a piano, playing it all out of time, and wrong notes – and know whether, somewhere in there, there's a hit song.'

Finally, in Jamaica, there are also women working in studios: lawyer Jahnet Enwright occasionally produces for Tuff Gong; Sonia Pottinger owns the late Duke Reid's Treasure Isle Studios and produced two Marcia Griffiths albums (under the name of S.E. Pottinger), as well as records by Junior Murvin, Judy Mowatt, Delroy Wilson, and others.

Many women in studios are still to be found doing the bookings or at reception, organizing sessions and staff rotas, and selling studio time; often, of course, they'll be doing the manager's job in all but title. However, increasing numbers *are* becoming involved in the technical side. And in the 1980s, as some of the old rock'n'roll myths creep out of fashion, more women will perhaps see these jobs as possibilities.

Women are still rare as club DJs. Neneh Cherry and Andrea (formerly of Rip, Rig, and Panic) working at The Bite Nite Club, London. (photo: Kerstin Rodgers)

CHAPTER FOUR

MEDIA MATTERS

SHERYL GARRATT

THE SAME OLD SHOW (ON YOUR RADIO)

Turn the dials, listen to your special, intimate friend, the DJ, who always sounds as if he were talking directly to you. Listen to Radio London. A paperboy has phoned into Tony Blackburn's morning soul show, and is asked if he reads 'page three'. Cue record: 'Ooh, I lurve you baybee'. A 'housewife' calls with a dedication, and is asked to twang her suspenders over the air. Twist the dial, and you're on Wonderful Radio One. The voice is telling me that I should buy this record if only to drool over the cover – the singer is such a sexy lady. Move again, and again, and every time, on every station, little but love songs, innuendo, and nonsense. Those reassuring male voices speaking only to you.

The theory – ridiculous in these days of high unemployment – is that the main audience for daytime radio are women listening-in while working at home, and that a woman's voice over the air would alienate them, shatter the illusion of a one-to-one relationship with the DJ. 'I don't go along with that,' said Anne Nightingale, for a long time Radio One's only female DJ.

It's assuming that no woman will get on with other women. Within six months, I was getting as many letters from women as from men, and I still do to this day, probably more. In the old days, they used to try to vamp me up a bit, make me out as some sort of sexy creature. And that's where it *would* be alienating to the audience, definitely. As long as all the listeners aren't thinking you're having a wild affair with Steve Wright, or something, you can actually communicate really easily.

When Radio One first started, the doors seemed closed to women like Anne, who ran a rock magazine-programme for BBC Radio Brighton. Their argument, she told Marion Fudger in *Spare Rib* 10 years ago, was based on a survey that showed that 'the public didn't like listening to women because they sounded hysterical, giggly, too upper-class or like fishwives, whereas men were preferred for their deep, reassuring, authoritative tones.' She dismissed the results, citing instead a survey carried out by the commercial stations, where subjects were asked if they liked the fact that a commentary had been done by a woman rather than a man: 'Over 80 per cent hadn't noticed!'

Today, she is less angry, and when asked why only Janice Long had since followed her with a national pop show, she firmly put the blame on women themselves:

The BBC will tell you that they get lots and lots of demo-tapes from blokes who want to be DJs, but from women they get none at all. Which is astounding. I get letters from girls of about 15 or 16 saying, 'I want to do what you do, but my parents think it's stupid – they want me to take a secretarial course.' And I'm sure they only want to be DJs because that way they can get to meet Duran Duran – I *know* Duran Duran fans' handwriting. But I think they do get put off by their parents. Janice Long is perfect material because she's not a school-leaver, she's had experience of life and of coping with people. I don't think I could have handled it if I was a lot younger, and yet Radio One is taking on 21-year-old DJs! I've been doing lectures for *Cosmopolitan* magazine, a one-day course on 'Women in Radio'. In the morning, they're shown interviewing techniques and how to work a tape-recorder, and then I go along and give them a pep-talk in the afternoon. There's been a terrific response to it – these women range from 18 to 60, but when I ask who wants to be a DJ, I get one out of 50. It's not an area they want to be involved in.

Janice Long, Radio One DJ, carefully posed for a press shot. (photo: BBC Picture Publicity)

The local radio stations also have few women pop DJs, with women still tending to gravitate towards 'soft' news, chat shows, and, of course, the women's programmes. 'I've fought that all along,' stated Anne firmly.

> I had to go in as the butch rock-jock! One day, many years ago, I played a request for a girl in Somerset, and she sent me a jar of homemade marmalade, so I said thank you over the air. And the technical op who was in the cubicle balancing the sound – your only immediate audience – said, 'Oh, we'll be having knitting-patterns next!' And I thought, 'That's it!' It doesn't work being cosy – women have to be almost *more* butch. Men can get away with doing knitting-patterns or exercises – Wogan used to do all that. But I didn't want to be shuffled into those sorts of areas, because once you're trapped in that, I don't think you ever get out.'

By the end of the 1980s, there will be around 85 Independent Local Radio (ILR) stations in need of presenters. Anne claims that 'they'd welcome more women, and would help them.' Otherwise, there are the hospital radio stations. Similarly, although the pirate stations no longer offer the mass exposure they could in the 1960s, they, too, can give women valuable experience. When Anne began at Radio One, it was with a group of men who, like Noel Edmunds, had all worked in pirate radio. Once more, women's problems with technology worked against them: 'Technically, it's terrifying. I had to be shown how to do it, and I found it very daunting. It's all about co-ordination, and mine isn't very good. But until you become automatic, it's very hard to relax your voice. And, of course, all the others had already learned from various ways.'

Surprisingly, there are far more women working on the technical side of radio than there are doing similar work in record studios. The BBC prefer to use their own technicians, and their desks are built slightly differently, leaving outside engineers momentarily disorientated. Rather than insisting on experience, they tend to recruit at colleges and train successful applicants from scratch, all of which has worked to women's advantage. But for women who want to be involved in the more visible, glamorous side of radio, Anne Nightingale offers this advice:

> I used to get a bit annoyed with things like 'Women In Media' screaming for jobs in radio. There's a lot of men screaming for jobs and not getting them. I don't think you *can* demand – you've got to plod away quietly and do the job as best you can. Eventually, they'll grudgingly give it to you, but you've got to be in the right place for a hell of a long time.

IN SEARCH OF THE BRIGHT YOUNG THING: POP ON TV

The greatest pop show ever was also one of the first, *Ready Steady Go!* – a programme that also had the perfect female presenter in Cathy McGowan. Cathy had all the qualities producers have looked for in vain ever since: she was young, pretty, immaculately hip, and, most of all, she was involved. The eternal breathless fan, Cathy chatted to the groups that were her peers with unselfconscious ease, and her only critical comments were variations on the same word: 'Smashing'. Her image still haunts the pop shows, and almost every female presenter since has, to some extent, been modelled on her.

The problem is that so often pop programmes are made by people who are totally outside the music scene. Desperate to make viewers feel involved, they try to pretend that the programme is made by people who *know* their lives. DJs are, of course, an obvious choice as presenters. Even these men who play and make the hits often find it impossible to sustain the illusion of a programme made for and by the young. *Top Of The Pops* has long been regarded as a family entertainment show, and assiduously avoids possible offence; Peter Powell's *Oxford Road Show* is more of a magazine than a music programme. But shows like the ill-fated *Switch*, or the more successful *Riverside* or *The Tube*, have to have their Bright Young Things to identify with The Kids. For women, especially, to be young, slim, attractive, and reasonably 'alternative' looking, is far more important than any musical knowledge or even a good camera technique.

The result is actress Lesley Ash of *The Tube* looking good but uncomfortable as she tries to interview bands she knows nothing about. The Midlands show *Look, Hear!* did a little better with their choice of Toyah Wilcox, a star herself and also an actress who was comfortable in the studio. Unfortunately though, interviewees had to fight hard to be glimpsed on screen, such was Ms Wilcox's overbearing presence. Meanwhile, Alison Short, whose involvement with record companies gives her a vast knowledge of the

Cathy McGowan (right) interviews Cilla Black on the prototype TV pop show, Ready Steady Go! (1964). (photo: Val Wilmer/Format)

industry and its workings, was turned down for a spot on *Riverside* because, at 32, she is too old.

A ray of hope came in the unlikely form of Paula Yates. In her last series of *The Tube*, she was no more knowledgeable or incisive than the rest, but at least she helped change the image expected by continuing to work throughout her pregnancy. Her last appearance on the show even seemed to be promoted on the idea that she might go into labour on the air (the press made much of the fact that an emergency ambulance would be on hand, just in case). Paula did us all a favour by being the first woman on TV not only to look glamorous all through her pregnancy, but to turn her imminent motherhood into a positive advantage.

On the other side of the camera, the position of women is no better than in any other area of TV; the lack of female camera operators, directors or producers throughout is well documented. Muriel Young produced many of the teeny-pop shows of the 1970s, including series featuring Marc Bolan, Child, and the Bay City Rollers' long-running *Shang-A-Lang*. She recently produced *Ladybirds*, a Mike Mansfield series for Channel 4, featuring female pop artists. So, although the role of a producer has changed and become more technical since the 1960s, it is still a surprise to discover that the producer of *Ready Steady Go!* was a woman – Vicki Wickham.

Vicki started on the show as a production assistant – traditionally a woman's job – but recalls that

> By the time it was on the air, I was either associate or assistant producer, by default. I knew nothing about music, nothing about TV, but, because there was no one else, when it went out live nine months later I was the producer. It was a *fait accompli* before they could prevent me. The show was working, I was already through the

Paula Yates, (left), continued to present 'The Tube' TV show throughout her much-publicized pregnancy in 1983. (photo: Tyne Tees Television)

> door and doing it, so nobody ever questioned whether I was a girl or not. My job was literally putting it all together: booking the show, putting all the elements in, writing it, having poor Cathy say, 'Smashing'. It was totally not planned. We all learned as we went, but because we didn't know, it worked. It was just being in the right place at the right time.

STICKS AND STONES

It's hard to remember now exactly what I expected when I first visited *NME*'s offices in Carnaby Street: I know I was disappointed. The general image of a music paper is of a high-tech, open-plan room, plastered with music and posters,

Famous People coming in and out, a lively exchange of news and ideas – all young, hip, and up to date. In fact, the atmosphere is usually hostile until you prove yourself, and many women just aren't pushy enough to get that far: they either haven't got the self-confidence, or they lack the ambition to go through it all just to be accepted in the end as 'one of the lads'. Female names may appear for a few months; some, such as Debbie Kirby, the editor of the weekly black music paper *Echoes* may reach positions of great influence. Few last for long, however. It is interesting that even some of the ones who do, turn out to be pseudonyms for men: the *NME*'s Susan Williams, for instance, is male ranting poet, Seething Wells.

Yet writing is a profession where women have a strong tradition, where lack of technical or mechanical knowledge does not restrict them, and where much of the work can even be done privately, at home. It is an ambition that can be seen as viable, even acceptable, for young women – although the boys' world of rock'n'roll isn't considered the most wholesome place to start. Above all, new young writers are positively welcomed by the music press. Experience isn't necessary and enthusiasm and ideas are often more important than any great literary talent; in theory, it's an ideal place to learn; in practice, things often work out differently.

Vivien Goldman, freelance journalist:

When I started, I was writing for *NME*, and you know the way they're theoretically on the lookout for good writers, encouraging you to develop, and so on. Well, they never did. I was too shy to really push myself forward like many of the men would have done. I thought that if they wanted me, they would ask for me, and if they weren't asking, it must be that I wasn't good enough.

But this lack of encouragement happens to all but the lucky few, male or female, as *Sounds* reviews editor, Robbi Millar, explained: 'I think it's just a case of them not liking anybody who might come in and steal a little of their glory, whatever that is. It's not just women, it's anybody

Journalist Vivien Goldman leaving New York's Studio 54 disco with Grace Jones. (photo: Adrian Boot, courtesy Vivien Goldman)

88

with anything interesting to say because, let's face it, none of them have got anything much.'

Again, the atmosphere can change rapidly according to the era: the NME I saw in 1980 was very different from the office Julie Burchill remembered from two years before, where she and journalist husband Tony Parsons had built their 'Kinderbunker' – a compartment edged with glass and barbed wire to keep out outsiders. In 1984, it is different again – younger, friendlier and less self-important now that the power of the older music press has been broken by glossy magazines such as Smash Hits. Now an editor of the London listings magazine City Limits, Penny Valentine was part of a small group of women who, in the 1960s, were an integral part of the pop scene. As singles reviewer (and the only woman) on Disc, she was promoted as a personality, an archetypal 'Swinging London Girl'. She laughs now as she recalls being asked for her autograph in the street. At that time, the fact that there were no women high up in the record companies was not even questioned. The women who did infiltrate 'male' areas weren't even considered curiosities or crusaders. Penny Valentine remembers those days:

Penny Valentine interviews Scott Walker, mid '60s.
(photo: courtesy Penny Valentine)

I was a fan, but I never saw it as being very important because, in the very early 1960s, music didn't have the same cultural significance that it does now. It hadn't been put into perspective, you just didn't realize that history was about to be made. It was just another job where you happened to meet people who made music, that was all. When I worked on Boyfriend, the Rolling Stones and the Beatles had just started, and I met them very much on the same level. None of us was aware of what was happening – them or us – it was on a kind of juvenile, fun level. So it didn't hit you as being very glamorous. At the time, it was incredibly innocent, really.'

By the 1970s, however, the music and the atmosphere had changed.

It was a different sort of era, and the emphasis had come off singles and shifted to albums. When I first started at Sounds, it seemed more adult, more grown up. The 'boys' were much more serious – about the music and themselves – and obviously I was finally growing up a bit as well.

In a few years, it stopped being fun. People started dealing with me in a very different way, and that was when I started to find it really hard to navigate my way being a woman, there's no doubt about that. There was an influx of American groups around that period who all thought that if you were a woman journalist, you were just ready for the sack. Another thing was that as music got more heavy rock, it became more macho-defined, whereas I don't think pop was very macho-defined. And the reasons for making music also changed: there were a lot of obvious manipulations going on which there hadn't been before. Record companies had changed, the whole basis of music had changed because people had realized you could make a lot of money out of it. So record companies got much bigger and more streamlined, full of accountants. The innocence of the music and the music business dropped, and so the innocence of the musicians dropped, and the whole thing changed colour.

This was the atmosphere encountered by Caroline Coon when she began to work on *Melody Maker* in the early 70s:

> One of the great disappointments for me, one of the things that I had presumed from the battles for liberation and the hippy movement of equality, was that the sex barriers had been broken down. It was horrible to find people who were lip-servicing 'the new world' still holding up unbelievably thick chauvinist barricades. You'd literally walk in the office and men would snigger because you were a woman.

Vivien Goldman found herself in a similar situation when she took a staff job at *Sounds*:

> It was the only paper that really had a lot of women writers – but all of them were either driven mad or kicked out, none of them lasted the course. I almost had a nervous breakdown. To go in there every day, you had to be wearing a suit of armour. I think it was my politics rather than my being a woman that was the main problem – they would try to trivialize and belittle women's politics as much as they could. There were a lot of tears in the ladies' loo, I remember. We were always hanging out there, the girls. You have to make sure that your work is really impeccable – you really do have to do it twice as well as a guy to get the same place, and even then, you are resented.

Vivien specialized in reggae, Caroline in star names and pop women such as Suzi Quatro, Olivia Newton-John and Lindsey de Paul – 'people whom no one else was going to touch with a barge-pole, whom everyone was trivializing' – as a way of avoiding bands like Yes, Led Zeppelin and the Eagles, whom she found 'boring and macho beyond words'. But then along came the music Caroline dubbed 'punk rock', and the press was once more transformed.

In the late 1970s, the new music and much of the writing that dealt with it became aggressive, violent, confrontational, and more self-consciously political. Fanzine writers would think nothing of striding into a dressing-room uninvited, slapping a tape-recorder down and demanding an interview. Access was rarely a problem, to be opinionated or outspoken was a virtue, and, often hiding behind pseudonyms, many of us were filled with an energy and arrogance that seems impossible now. Lucy Toothpaste (Lucy Whitman) wrote and printed some of the first feminist comments on the music in *Jolt*; in Birmingham, a group of women wrote *Brass Lip*; Vinyl Virgin and friend were producing *Moron*. Girls everywhere were writing in messy, cheaply printed 'zines. In the music press, Jane Suck was becoming notorious at *Sounds*. Even more controversial was the young Bristol girl who mouthed off in *NME* every week: Julie Burchill.

> I sent in a review of a Patti Smith album – I didn't know it had to be typed, so I just wrote it down on school notepaper, and, of course, that drove them mad! They loved the idea of someone of 16 writing like that, they thought it was really exotic. And I got the job.
>
> I was very, very shy, and I played the punk role to the hilt, because it was something to hide behind. To complement this new, nasty image, Tony [Parsons]

brought me a huge black switchblade from France, and I would sit in the office flicking it open at opportune moments and cleaning my nails with it. I think they were appalled by that, but I got away with it because that was the way they thought a punk was supposed to act. Looking back on it, they gave me an amazing amount of freedom, and because I was a punk with like a capital 'P', because I had this larger-than-life image, that just covered up my sex. Tony and I were always treated in exactly the same way.'

But has being female ever caused any problems?

No. You're different, people remember you more. I'm not sure if that's true of all female writers, but I could get away with a lot more. I could be ruder to people and they wouldn't take offence so quickly, they'd think, 'Oh, it's just one of her little ways.' I *was* condescended to because I was so young and all, but that never really bothered me because it gives you a chance to creep up behind them. If someone under-rates you, you can give them a few shocks. I think it's quite a good thing.

Vivien Goldman has more mixed feelings:

On one level, people are more open to you because you're just a girl and so it doesn't matter, and, on another level, they just don't take you seriously. My most famous incident was in interview I had with Peter Tosh that I wrote up in this big thing for *Melody Maker*. We had such a set-to, with him saying that women are the channel of the devil, a blazing row that was all on tape.

Both Robbi Millar and Caroline Coon spoke of similar encounters with rock bands, but felt that at times their gender could also be an advantage in interviews. Often, they claim, people tend to trust women more, the social games between men and women are so much more easy and established. Vivien Goldman is quick to point out, however, that gender can also be used against you:

When I got friendly with Denise Mills, who manages Black Uhuru, she said there was something she'd been dying to know, then asked if it was true that I'd slept with this whole list of reggae musicians, from Big Youth to Burning Spear to Yellowman. I mean, who'd *want* to sleep with all those guys? In this business, there *does* get to be an overlap socially between your work and your life, but that's not the point. It's another way that guys will use to trivialize your work. They will use any excuse to say you're only in it because you're a groupie.

Val Wilmer moved between several musical worlds:

It was noticeable that in the rock world, interviews were fixed up as a matter of course, but in the jazz world, where I had to fix my own, a double stereotyping was in operation. Most of the jazz people were black and the prevailing racist assumption was that they could offer a white woman nothing but sex and their music. And at the same time, a white woman could only be there for sex, too. It never entered their minds that *I* could be interesting in my own right.

People stopped me getting backstage to see the musicians, stopped me going to hotels, prevented me having access to interview musicians: that's what hurt me most. That kind of attitude hasn't stopped to this day, which really surprises me. It didn't stop when I came out as a lesbian, nor did it stop as I got older and, therefore – according to the standard thing – less attractive to men. Also I had a name, a reputation. But at 42 years of age, it still happens to me. Of course, they don't stand in the way so much, but they still sneer.

Yet women writers have become more acceptable, and Lesley White, an editor of *The Face*, expressed surprise that so few women approach her with ideas. Women are not taught to ask for what they want, and although men, too, are often shy or vulnerable, women's fear of rejection is almost crippling. It is easy to get disheartened; afraid of failure, we often avoid trying at all. Julie Burchill gave her advice to girls who want to write:

> Unless you're very lucky, like I was, you just have to keep bashing away at it, sending in stuff which nine times out of ten won't get used. That doesn't *seem* very glamorous or promising, but it's the way most people get into it. Neil Spencer [editor of the *NME*] is not going to appear at your front door on a magic carpet one night and whisk you off to Carnaby Street.

When Vivien Goldman became acting features editor on *Sounds*, she had to overcome a typical lack of assertiveness to have her position recognised:

> It took months – with Caroline Coon's help – to realize that I *was* features editor, not acting, because nobody else was doing it. This is a very important thing, I think, this timidity. I was too timid to push myself to get more writing on *NME*, too timid to push myself for what I knew I really wanted. I kept thinking that they would ask me. Then one day, I pinned the editor Alan Lewis against the wall and said, 'Listen, I've been acting features editor for months now,

you've got me doing it for the same salary as a writer, and it's just not on. Look around, I may not be that good, but who's better?' So in the end I became features editor. And after I'd done it for a while, I did have a certain reputation and people couldn't shit on me that much. That was after years, though. When I went freelance, I decided I wanted nothing more to do with office politics and I'd rather have less money. I just couldn't deal with it. You are very isolated if you're in there working. They just don't like women and women's ways in the office.

Secretaries, especially, are not well treated, as Julie Burchill pointed out:

> We used to hang around a lot with the office staff at *NME*, and that annoyed them a lot. The writers thought we were drawing attention to the way they treated them, which was quite shabby in those days. The rest of the writers thought we were being really funny, that we were slumming. But we just found the secretaries more entertaining: we used to have some real laughs.

Out of all the women interviewed, only Lesley White felt at ease in her magazine's offices. Again, things seem to be changing. Photographer Janette Beckman, who has moved from London to New York, was optimistic:

> I find these days that the bands I have to deal with are a lot softer, less macho, except among the heavy metal fraternity, of course! Just checking out the likes of Wham!, Style Council, Culture Club, ABC, Heaven 17, the Thompson Twins and Michael Jackson, to name a few, the more effete look and manners for boys is *in*, sexism is *out*, in England at least. There has been a definite improvement since I started working in the

industry – I always had a lot of trouble in England relating to the 'one of the lads' syndrome. Here in New York I have a much better reaction from art directors and press people. They seem to treat everyone equally, and I get the feeling that they tend to judge your work, not you. It only remains for the journalists to catch up, and as the young blood comes in and more of the old guys from the 1970s era retire, things could be on the up and up.

The press seems to be more open to women photographers; and Pennie Smith, Lynn Goldsmith, Jill Furmanowsky, are among some of the others at the top.

The 1980s do seem more relaxed, and magazines such as *Smash Hits* and *No.1* appear to have a friendlier atmosphere than the self-obsessed rock press of the 1970s. Once again, pop is largely trivial and meaningless, and although professional, the new glossy mags avoid criticism or intellectual analysis. It is impossible for the staff to take themselves too seriously, and it is interesting that Lynn Hanna and Deanne Pearson – two women who left the rock press after becoming fairly established there – have both re-emerged in the offices of *No.1*. Whether this more open mood will last is impossible to say. As Lesley White pointed out, very little of it is in the control of the women themselves:

I think my experience at *The Face* is very much to do with the fact that I happen to be working with people who are nice, sensitive, and not particularly exploitative. Which is awful in a way: it's not written into my contract or anything, and it means that if they *weren't* like that, I'd have no protection whatsoever. I'm sure that's what a lot of women who work with men have to rely on – the blokes' good nature.

But there have also always been women involved no matter what the climate, continuing to inspire and support each other. As Caroline Coon says: 'You are a woman working in a man's world, and you can't let it get you down. And it got better when I met other women like Viv: we were a little team, a little posse, and, quite frankly, we were having a wonderful time!'

Rock photographer Lynn Goldsmith, also known as musical agony uncle Will Powers, poses for her own camera.
(photo: Lynn Goldsmith, courtesy Island Records)

CHAPTER FIVE

VOICES OF WOMEN

SUE STEWARD

Sandie Shaw:

I used to sing at Dagenham dance halls and youth clubs from about 13. The guys were all imitating Cliff and the Shadows, and I used to sing the American songs. One day there was a talent contest at the Palais. *I* thought I was a better dancer, but my mates thought I should go in for the singing contest. I didn't win, but somebody came up to me afterwards and asked me to go to town for an audition. I thought he was taking the piss, but I went – all on my own. They showed me into this room with a piano! I'd never sung with a piano before – I couldn't utter a note. But for some reason they just took everybody's word for it that I could sing – probably I just *looked* right. They asked me to rehearse with a local band and put me on a Charity Show with the Hollies and Adam Faith. I did one number and ran off. My aunt Jean said, 'Go and have a port, Sandra,' and as I ran past the Hollies said, 'Go on, you're fantastic.' I thought they were taking the piss. I was still at school and they were megastars!

I ended up being dragged into Adam Faith's dressing-room, and he asked me to sing. I was so nervous I just clammed up. Next door was his manager, Eve Taylor. He grabbed her and said, 'You gotta listen to this girl.' She said, 'Oh, really,' and walked out!

For the next few weeks while Adam tried to persuade Eve how wonderful I was, I went to Ford's to work. When I eventually went to see Eve, I took my boyfriend, and my mum and dad. I actually signed a contract without a lawyer, without advice and without reading it. Eve still hadn't heard me sing.

(photo: SKR photo/LFI)

THE SINGER, NOT THE SONG

As Sandie Shaw's story suggests, it is often the woman herself – not necessarily her voice – which will get her the part. Singers have a double function in a band: they are a focus both through the words they sing, and via their looks; primarily, they must be a good-looking crowd-puller. Hence, the relative ease with which women become singers. Behind the adulation paid to a good performer, though, there is an attitude which takes the expressive and emotional capacities of women singers for granted. After all, women are expected to show some emotion. Part of this attitude comes from the knowledge that we all have a voice, though most are rusty and unusable. Because most of us could sing some sort of thread of notes, singing is assumed to be an easy option – or at least easier than playing a 'real' instrument. Within a rock group, the singer's status is frequently lower than the instrumentalists' – particularly if the singer is female. Passable-to-good singers are two a penny and often, after a brief flirtation with fame, they are unceremoniously dumped into cabaret or ignominy. It can be a cruel occupation. Nevertheless, along with dancing, it still maintains its rags-to-riches myth of ordinary life transformed into fame and stardom through the voice. More women become singers than anything else in pop music. But the majority of women in this country hardly ever sing outside their bathroom, the kitchen (to the radio), to their children, or on special church occasions. Unlike the tribal male sing-songs at football matches, women's singing tends to be private and individual. Gone is the community tradition of singing as a form of weekend family entertainment – the sort of background that both Cilla Black and Lulu came from. (Though it does persist in Caribbean communities, where the expressive participatory church worship has produced many fine lovers'-rock singers (Carroll Thompson, Jean Adebambo, Janet Kay) as well as back-up singers who may later move on to solo careers.)

Ranking Ann, toaster with the London-based Ariwa Posse Roadshow:

> It started when I got interested in reggae. I tended to play the dub [B-side, instrumental] sides of records, and as I listened I found I could add words to it. I was creating lyrics that flowed naturally and then I was 'toasting' away to myself in my little front room. It got to the stage where I was putting it on tape and other people were liking it. My brother's got a sound system and I used to go along with him. So one day I thought I'd get on the mike and see how it felt. I didn't have a lot of lyrics then – the first time was just a couple of lines all the way through the record. But it felt good doing it and it just grew from there.

Toasters nearly always speak over pre-recorded rhythms, but many women, like Ranking Ann, remember getting started through singing along to records; partly drawing on some awareness of tradition, partly emulating established female singers. Singing is *the* age-old option for women. Consequently, there is a rich variety of styles, each with its own clear-cut lineage. Eras are identifiable as much by prevailing vocal styles as by instruments or dress. Blues singers have been an all-time major influence on rock voices. Bessie Smith and Mama Thornton were the revered inspiration of Janis Joplin who, in turn, affected a great number of women in Britain – from Maggie Bell's tougher, Glaswegian style, to the slightly softer, though no less soulful, tones of Christine Perfect and Carol Grimes. It is ironic that, 10 years later, Kim Carnes and Bonnie Tyler should both have achieved international fame with voices which are at times indistinguishable (presumably by design) from one of the best of the white male 1960s blues imitators, Rod

Ranking Ann (photo: Anna Arnone)

chance to perform solo and an independence they would never have been offered on the rock circuit. The folk-club scene was the grounding for many women in rock – right up to the present-day crop of young women musicians, including those, like Lesley Woods of the Au Pairs, in punk bands. It was also the route for 1960s women like Sandy Denny and Maddy Prior, who later made careers in electric folk-rock. Another reason for this affinity between folk and women is the style's emphasis on lyrics. Schoolgirls have a tendency to poesy and introspection, and often keep notebooks of poems and jottings – which are really only one step removed from song lyrics.

Initially most folk-singers accompanied themselves with an acoustic guitar, and sang in pure, schoolgirl choir voices. As the music developed, some moved away from that stereotype and used their voices like a folk-rock instrument, adding more colour, taking the part of the drone or variant melody-line. All the well-known folk-rock bands during the early 1970s were fronted by a female singer with a powerful voice, and an equally strong and autonomous identity within the band.

The US equivalents of folk clubs were the coffee shops. The Greenwich Village scene launched Joan Baez, Joni Mitchell, Judy Collins, Maria Muldaur, and even Janis Joplin – though she soon moved off into more 'authentic' blues cellars. Joan Baez and Joni Mitchell were easily the most influential singers on that scene. Joni Mitchell eventually rejected folk's naturalistic style to experiment more individually with her voice. Even in the early days it was characterized by the jazz-singer/instrumental qualities that mark it today: a jagged, eccentric sense of melody; a switchback of highs and lows.

Similarly, Patti Smith influenced the idiosyncratic vocal styles of 1970s white female singers. Looking for a way of reading her poems to music,

Stewart. More recently, Alison (Alf) Moyett, formerly of Yazoo and now solo, was profoundly influenced by blues singers, too.

Even while the blues held sway, the route into pop music for many women was through folk music. During the 1960s, every town had a folk club which served as an ideal launching-pad for mainly middle-class women: a kind of licensed half-way house between the church choir and electric rock band. Such venues gave girls a

Patti Smith   (photo: Shirley O'Loughlin)

Patti developed the distinctive half-spoken, half-sneered monotone, intercepted by yelps, that eventually evolved into 'true singing'. Though obviously not every female singer sang in this style, it was a formula that formed the basis of the punk era. There are still quite a few dyed-in-the-wool punkettes, like the Gymslips, who preserve that original style; most, however, have moved on to some kind of individuality or disappeared altogether. Siouxsie, who began with the monotoned version of The Lord's Prayer, has become a more conventional singer – albeit using a style that often hovers closer to speech than to conventional ideas of a sung melody. Her warbling banshee voice has influenced many other singers (e.g. Elizabeth Frazer of the Cocteau Twins), though its similarity to the sound of women like Nina Hagen and Bettina Koster

(Malaria, Germany) seems to be a case of parallel development, rather than direct influence. It is amusing that early Siouxsie songs recall Grace Slick's psychedelic soarings with the 1960s West Coast band, Jefferson Airplane.

Pop music's history is a series of influences, both backwards in time, and sideways into other kinds of music. Singers particularly reveal this process: Brenda Lee's absorption of the r'n'b idiom through LaVern Baker's and Ruth Brown's hits; Dinah Washington was a friend of Aretha Franklin's church-centred family and had the greatest influence on Aretha's voice; while Randy Crawford's typical deep-soul style reveals debts to Bettye Swann's lovely 'Southern Soul' flutter. Moving on from the 1950s to the 1960s, we find Cilla Black and Sandie Shaw borrowing intonations and phrasing wholesale from Dionne Warwick and Lesley Gore. In the 1980s, Mari Wilson has picked up on (and, in the process, inspired a rediscovery of) Julie London, while the Eurythmics' Annie Lennox reveals *her* 1960s soul heroines – particularly through the arrangements of Eurythmics' songs, which pitch her against the horn section and back-up singers, à la Dionne Warwicke or Martha Reeves 20 years earlier. The influence of gospel singers is particularly noticeable in Helen Terry's expansive soarings and Alison Moyett's rich outpourings. The current country and rockabilly revivals make connections between the 1950s rockabilly women and a cast of contemporary country-clad gals – Helen (McCookerybook) and the Horns, Fiona (singer with Yip Yip Coyote) and the Shillelagh Sisters. Chryssie Hynde's voice has always betrayed signs of the tear-jerking breaks which make country singers like Dolly Parton and Crystal Gayle so irresistible.

When women talk of their idols and influences, as often as not they tell stories about singing along with records, trying to copy someone's voice – at least until they can begin to develop their own style. Lotti Golden is today a New York electro-funk producer. Her musical career began when she was 14, as 'a chick singer with a rock band':

> I would practise singing to Aretha, Ray Charles, the Marvellettes, till I could sing all their licks and runs. I practised controlling my vibrato every day for hours, until my throat muscles would know how to produce that great 'do-op' vibrato. And the girls' bathroom in high school was a great place to try it out!

Helen Terry is one of the most soulful white singers on the English recording scene today:

> I go through 'getting ready to do vocals' moods, listening to lots of different vocalists

Success story for a session singer: Helen Terry found her solo voice in 1984 after years of backing other people.
(photo: courtesy Virgin Records)

in different styles. I do it to get into the skill of singing, as it were, listening for things like phrasing and fluidity – Sarah Vaughan is *so* fluid . . .

A lot of women, Helen Terry among them, find themselves singing back-up vocals. This is undoubtedly a useful route to solo success for many. The recent fashion for using two or three singers to supplement an ordinary white pop solo voice (usually male) has focused attention on several young black singers in Britain. Both Carol Kenyon and D.C. Lee have moved relatively quickly, from working behind Style Council and Wham! respectively, to working solo. There is sometimes a tendency to dismiss back-up singers, but they can have an important colouring function: their harmonies can transform a rather lifeless and one-dimensional arrangement into a rich and lively song. For the women involved, the work serves as a vital access route to a solo career, as American soul singer Patti Austen explained in *Black Echoes*, in March, 1983: 'It's not a derogatory or low-class kind of thing to do. It's the best education you can get; when you learn that way, things get imprinted on your brain.' Unfortunately, for many it's a frustrating beginning and end of the line; always someone else's back-up, never their own lead. But as a consolatory afterthought, Linda Ronstadt once claimed that she liked doing back-ups because she could relax and enjoy singing, 'There's no pressure, it's like a vacation' (*Let it Rock* 1975).

Because it is an established position for women to fill, singing can be a restriction. Sometimes it is difficult for them to enter other areas or, indeed, to move from one genre to another. Dee Dee Bridgewater started out as a jazz singer (working with bands as varied as Dizzy Gillespie, Roland Kirk, Roy Ayers). When she wanted to move into rock music in the 1980s, she found her way blocked. In *Black Music* (1981), she

related:

I really like rock music and when the time came to make the album, they were saying, 'Who do you want to produce you and what do you want to do?' I said I wanted to do rock'n'roll 'cos I enjoy all the high energy of rock . . . it symbolizes rebellion . . . So I said that's what I want to do, and I'd like the Doobie Brothers to produce. They couldn't believe it . . . 'Dee Dee, er . . . you're black and . . . Dee Dee, be serious now.' I couldn't do it because I was black.

She had to agree to use one of the top black disco producers, Thom Bell, instead. Making it as a solo artist, on your own terms, can be difficult. However, there are some styles which have enabled women to do some very positive things with their voices, often exploiting those very qualities that are dismissed *because* they are female.

RAP, SCAT AND TOAST

A theme running through pop music is a combination of street-talk, girls' talk, and women's conversations about love's ups and downs, complexities and unfairnesses. In the USA, rapping, a sung-spoken style, is deep-rooted in black music. Every few years, there's a new revival in a new guise. The late 1970s revamp was proudly macho – all sexual boasts and challenges and come-ons – and the rapping itself was accompanied by the latest manifestation of 'all city boys together' chauvinism – break-dancing. Although there weren't many women rappers, there were some: the exuberant female trio, the Sequence, rapped *their* catalogue of star signs, tastes and occupations alongside the other Sugarhill gangs. They were good, smart and fast and easy entertainers, but rap was clearly a fad for them and they eventually switched to tight soul harmonies with an occasional nostalgic rap number in between. In 1984 the New York duo, Two Sisters, had a minor dancefloor hit with their rapped warning, 'B-boys Beware!' but the rest of the EP was straight singing.

The early 1970s rap style had been a more continuous, often a deeply heartfelt, outburst. Several of the soul raps were outlets for biting comments on men–women relationships, often pinned down to specific situations which most women (and most men of course) would painfully or amusedly recognize. Millie Jackson is Queen Rapper. Her boasts and explicit sexual counselling go all the way, leaving the men in the audience with their tails between their legs one minute and, confusingly, aroused the next; the women find themselves temporarily but hysterically vindicated and reassured. Millie is a man-killer, the aim of her gory stories is strictly below the belt. A few years earlier, the genre had been enlivened by Laura Lee. In 1970 she advised her sisters that 'Wedlock is a Padlock' they should avoid and, a year later, read them their 'Women's Love Rights'. While Millie's love triangles were specific, Laura Lee's advice and complaints were more general which ultimately made her more threatening and probably accounts for her being less well known today.

A popular version of the gender-war theme is the conversation rap, immortalized in Shirley Brown's telephone conversation – with 'the other woman': in her classic eternal-triangle hit song, 'Woman to Woman', which revolved around love, jealousy and rivalry. It was Barbara Mason's 1984 chart hit, 'Another Man', which updated the theme: *her* husband is having an affair with another man . . . and so the classic rap format came back to the dance-floor.

In Jamaican music, a near equivalent to rap is another sung-spoken style known as toasting. A smattering of women – Sister Nancy in Jamaica, Shani Benjamin and Ranking Ann in England – rhyme their comments on women's lives, and on specific personal subjects, with a reggae backing-track. Sister Nancy's career as a car mechanic is the basis of her song 'Transport Connection'; Ranking Anne's *Slice of Toast* album featured *the* indictment of English racism, 'Don't Call Me No English Girl', and her smarting defence of feminism, 'Liberated Woman'.

Toasts aren't broken up into verses like the New York raps – they are more conversational and anecdotal, in the same vein as the extended soul raps of Millie Jackson and Laura Lee.

Like soul-rapping, toasting is often used to tell stories. Louise Bennett ('Miss Lou') is a Jamaican poet, folklorist and revered scholar, who recites Caribbean parables and myths in patois and frequently takes satirical swipes at white attitudes to 'local English', both in Jamaica and Britain. She reminds, educates and entertains young West Indians, presenting their own rich culture against a seductive background of calypso, mento or reggae. Miss Lou's exuberant and bubbly performances are characterized by long, involved 'parables' that are both attractive as songs *and* stirring polemic; there's hardly any difference between the lilting way she speaks and her 'singing'.

Billie Holiday called *her* voice a horn. In jazz, the voice has always functioned as an instrument, though it wasn't until the bebop era (1940s and 1950s) that scat solos came to have the same status as the other instruments; also at this time, scat singing began to mingle imperceptibly with them, particularly with the horns. Scatting has a long line of women in its history – from Ella Fitzgerald, Anita O'Day and Betty Carter in the States, to Cleo Laine, Sheila Jordan and Annie Ross in Britain. When Cleo Laine scats alongside Johnny Dankworth's saxophone, the leaps and turns each makes are so beautifully co-ordinated that it's like listening to dancing.

Scatting dispenses with true words altogether, and relies on the power of the sound, the rhythm-breaks, and the inflections. US-based Brazilian singers Flora Purim and Tania Maria have taken the style into new directions with their Latin-jazz-funk fusions. Tania Maria's voice flies off in a fast flurry of effervescent fragments, chasing or following the light runs of her electric keyboards. On record, where she can multitrack her voice, she often creates a sound like a sublime cluster of bursting saxophones.

A small number of European and American singers, who trace their roots to jazz and free improvisation, use scatting as part of their usually wordless style and vocabulary. This form of scatting draws on an astute understanding of the way women talk, listen and interact with each other, as well as a virtuoso voice control. Diamanda Galas is a Greek-American singer who uses her tremendous range and discipline to spine-tingling effect in vocal 'sketches', commentaries and observations. In performance, she uses special-effects, microphones and pre-recorded

Maggie Nicols (left) with r 'n b singer, Carol Grimes.
(photo: Pam Isherwood/Format)

tapes to exaggerate and project the rush of voices which, though expressing no true words, grip the audience just as firmly as if she had delivered a soap-box plea.

In England, Maggie Nicols and Julie Tippetts set up lighter scenarios through their adaptations of scatting. Their duets are frequently hilarious, sometimes painfully or embarrassingly familiar, but always provoking. As well as using the sounds and rhythms of speech, they also blend whole phrases, clichés, exaggerated facial expressions, gestures and snippets of conversations, with bursts of fragmented songs which every woman in the audience would recognize. The ingredients aren't for mocking, they're not to be dismissed as 'stupid girls' talk' or 'just' women gossiping, they are a calculated and often tongue-in-cheek exhibition of the particular way women and girls talk to each other. Their song 'Rabbiting' (on the *Sweet and S'Ours* LP) is a suitably over-the-top example of the style. In a roundabout way, they are very close to the form of pop music current in the 1960s, with girl groups' conversational songs: the Shangri-Las confiding in each other, bitching and gossiping – 'Is She Really Going Out With Him?'; the Crystals' progress reports back to their friends after a date – 'And Then He Kissed Me'. Girls' talk made public. Songs which could be written from the conversations of any of the girls walking down the street, arms linked – the kinds of song they'd be singing, oblivious to the rest of the world. Which is how most of the girl groups started out . . .

HIGH AND LOWS

As well as experimenting with content, some women use pitch to subvert expectations about femininity. There is no such thing as a 'natural' singing voice. It is affected by the same factors which shape our speech and accents, and each kind of music has tight conventions. As an

Julie Tippetts, '60s blues singer in her new jazz and improvising guise: Bracknell Jazz Festival, 1982. (photo: Pam Isherwood/Format)

instrument, the human voice is amenable to a whole range of styles. However, within that, there is obviously a difference between the voice of a small girl and that of a woman. The child stars whose innocent, pure voices bring them to popularity and fame are frequently forced to maintain that style as long as possible (just as they are forced to conceal their changing womanly bodies in bindings and girlish clothes).

Shirley Goodman was half of the 1950s US r'n'b team Shirley and Lee, whose hit songs included 'Let The Good Times Roll' and 'I Feel Good'. Shirley's screechy nasal vocals were a definite hook for their songs. On the sleeve of a recent compilation, *The Best of Shirley and Lee* (Ace), Shirley spilled the beans about how the record company made her retain that voice artificially: 'I consider it as a gimmick. I'd try and imitate

Dinah Washington and attempt a phrase as she would, but Aladdin [her original record company] always kept me singing high.' Shirley's influence, like so many other 1950s US r'n'b singers, was felt in Jamaica, on the voice of another early-teens girl, Millie Small. Her song, 'My Boy Lollipop' topped the UK charts in 1964, exhibiting the same squeaky, scratchy, little-girl style.

Marianne Faithfull, another 1960s figure, illustrated how the same vocal texture can be reinterpreted to fit the singer's image. Beginning as 'an innocent convent girl' with a breathy, wide-eyed schoolgirl's voice, she later 'became' hard and whisky-sodden with a voice to match. The style had been changed to keep up with her public image of hard-living woman.

Some child singers have women's voices. Most of the original rockabilly singers were around 14 years old, many of them starting out as radio stars. Their raw, abrasive voices matched their tough and 'tomboyish' style. Brenda Lee's voice was so powerful and mature at 14 that a rumour went about in France that she was an opportunistic midget posing as a little girl. Helen Shapiro remembers going to an audition in school uniform to prove that she really was a young girl!

The voice is super-adaptable, and can be made to add or subtract years. There are plenty of stories of women working in bands being encouraged – or directed – to sing high, in addition to those who positively choose this option. Kate Bush actually makes her voice sound like a little girl's by forcing it up to a higher register, as she describes in *Sound International* (September, 1980):

> I used to find it fascinating to write in a note that I couldn't reach and then a week later I'd got my throat into the shape where it could actually reach that note. It wasn't actually acrobatics that I was playing with. It was just that the songs I was writing –

they seemed to leap, that was what I wanted them to do, just fly in the air and be high.

Lene Lovich's squeaky, mobile aeronautics – which occasionally flicker into a yodel – are evocative of Eastern European women's folk-singing. She also seems to coincide occasionally, incidentally, with the explorations of jazz and avant-garde vocalists like Annette Peacock, Maggie Nicols and Yoko Ono. All are characterized by free-flying expressiveness, sudden mood-changes interspersed with bouts of conventional singing.

Perhaps it was a reaction against the tradition of girlish highs, and a nostalgic fascination with Astrud Gilberto's sultry, sensual, samba voice from the 1960s, which led Alison Stratton (Weekend) and Tracey Thorn (Everything but the Girl, Working Week), to their 1980s samba-revival style. Some women 'switch gender' altogether. Grace Jones exaggerated her naturally deep voice to match her new square-headed androgyny. Her earlier disco releases reveal a not-so-male voice (though not high, either) just as her earlier modelling shots show a not-so-male body. The new effect gave her a far more distinctive sound – and hit records. Others 'switch gender' electronically: US photographer Lynn Goldsmith became the deep-voiced agony uncle Will Powers, whose naive platitudes made a minor dint on the pop scene in 1983 with *Dancing for Mental Health*. Similarly, Laurie Anderson uses a Synclavier – 'half-electronic, half-human', as she described it – to comment on passing Americana. A mixture of taped interviews involving real-life characters and new 'characters' conjured from her own electronically treated voice. Laurie Anderson's 'songs' don't follow the standard pattern of verse, chorus, instrument-break. Nevertheless, her electronic telephone-tale 'Oh Superman!' was a surprising chart hit, and launched her career in the more lucrative waters of pop – always open to the occasional one-off novelty record from an experimentalist.

The voice operates as both a physical instrument *and* as a communicator of ideas, through song lyrics. The immense subject of women as song-writers and as the dominant subject of pop songs, is still virtually undocumented. Song lyrics affect and shape and influence women's perceptions of their lives, their relationships and their expectations. They are taken most seriously by young girls when they are most impressionable. The lyrics of country music songs are the key to the success of singer-songwriters like Tammy Wynette and Loretta Lynn, who put to music the experiences and feelings of millions of ordinary women, who buy their records. Mary Bufwack and Robert Oermann in Nashville have written several perceptive analyses of country music lyrics (see booklist), while Aida Pavletich's *Sirens of Song* is a much chattier, fascinating overview of the many departments of pop music and their female singing inhabitants. Simon Frith's writings for *New Society* and *Let it Rock* in the 1970s, are still pertinent and provocative discussions about the power and meaning of pop song lyrics for their listeners – and performers.

As a music lover who tends to hear music in abstracts and sometimes only becomes aware of words after years of listening, or when someone else points them out to me, I eagerly await updated and comprehensive treatment of the subject – including that period of the late 1970s when writers like Poly Styrene were breaking every rule in Tin Pan Alley's guidebook to songwriting, and endearing themselves to listeners all over Britain.

Tracey Thorn of the Everything but the Girl duo represents a new interest in the sultry, sensual quality of samba singing.
(photo: Peter Anderson, courtesy of Blanco y Negro records)

I love the sound of the sax, but I think it was David Bowie's brown zoot-suit and carroty hair — and sax — in his *Pin-up* days, that did it. I thought I could look as cool as that! Everyone kept saying it's an odd thing for a girl to do, but it never occurred to me. — Clare Hurst, Belle Stars   (photo: Anna Arnone)

CHAPTER SIX

CALLING THE TUNE

SUE STEWARD

WHOLE LOTTA PLAYIN' GOING' ON

About a year after Poison Girls started, I realized the traps of being a front-woman. When you stand there and do your singing bit, that's all right. But then there's an instrumental-break, and what do you do? Glamour, pout, dance . . . I felt extremely uncomfortable with all that, so I decided to learn to play the guitar . . . I learned very quickly!

— Vi Subversa, Poison Girls

I wanted to start an all-women's band and we formed Amazulu. At first I was managing them, but I used to go to the rehearsals and jam on the congas and pick up things and play, so when they went on stage, they would drag me on and make me do it there, too. I've never been to a class, I just play along to records on percussion – and recently I've started mucking around on the drums – we swap about.

— Sharon Bailey, Amazulu

The reasons why girls choose one instrument to play rather than another are just as random and unpredictable as they are for boys. In the end, it comes down to a personal preference for one sound over another. Beyond this, though, several 'hard' factors – class, education, race, physique and even geography – also affect their choices, and the chances of success. Instruments are not neutral objects, either: some have strong associations which can put potential girl players off. Although the exclusion of women from playing music is mostly informal, in some countries certain instruments are unavailable to them.

In Nigeria, for example, playing the talking drum (the rhythm backbone to juju pop music) is a skill handed down from father to son and withheld from girls. In many countries, flutes are widely considered to be men's instruments and sometimes women aren't even allowed to see them being played. Drums, too, can be invested with sacred values and are frequently used in religious ceremonies restricted to men. Western pop and rock have analogous taboos: girls are effectively kept away from electronics, guitars, and particularly drums; some girls are simply told, 'Only boys do that.' Discouragement like this may be just the incentive some girls need. The American folksinger Peggy Seeger, who comes from a well-known musical family, was warned away from the banjo with that line. So, of course, she took up the banjo. And later on, she wrote the classic anthem to female determination: 'I Want to be an Engineer'. More insidious is the fact that many of the instruments that girls *do* play – piano and violin, for instance – don't carry the same power and social excitement as, say, the electric guitar.

Some obstacles facing women are subtler and specific to music. For example, buying an instrument. The standard music equipment shop is a typically intimidating boys' club atmosphere. Men use these shops to show off their bedroom-practised solos along with their knowledge of technicalities and gadgets. Supercilious attendants will snigger audibly if a woman asks to test an instrument. They tend to assume you're there to buy your boyfriend's plectrums. But women's disadvantage as instrumentalists starts within the restrictive institutional environment of school.

MUSIC LESSONS

Music is not a fixed part of the curriculum in English junior schools: the amount and quality taught depends on the skill and interest of the staff, as well as the money available to buy instruments. For most kids, 'music' is singing around the piano, and, if they are lucky, 'percussion' is banging out rhythms on homemade instruments, triangles and tambourines. Better-

A music workshop being led by members of the mainly women reggae band, Abacush. (photo: Anna Arnone)

off schools pay someone to come in and teach piano, flute, cello to those *whose parents wish it*. If there are a lot of West Indian children in the school, there might be a steel-band class. But *the junior school instrument is the recorder*, presumably because it is cheap, light, small, and relatively easy to play. It is also a 'girls' instrument'. Susan Pidgeon, a London deputy-head teacher, reports: 'Very few boys seem to learn the recorder, they play football instead. The lessons are usually at lunchtime or after school, and the boys *tend* to go out, while the girls *tend* to prefer to stay in.'

Middle-class girls learn piano, violin, cello or flute – partly as a hangover from the days when it was desirable for potential wives to possess such accomplishments, and also because these instruments are central to the middle-class classical music tradition. Though schoolday music lessons rarely have any bearing on later life, these early, enforced piano lessons can unwittingly set girls on course for a future career in pop or rock.

At secondary schools, music is a serious subject, with exams and grades. Girls separate into factions: those who listen to, drool over and dance to pop, but don't play it; and the 'musicians', who join the school orchestra and very self-consciously and often snootily reject pop. There is little in a girl's environment outside school to counteract these negative influences, though regional variations in what girls are taught in school may offer different possibilities later on.

play version of the trumpet. Annie Whitehead's career in rock, pop, and jazz was grounded in that way:

> I come from Oldham in Lancashire, where there's a strong brass-band tradition. Every school's got one and they give you lessons. I wanted to play tuba at first, but they wouldn't let me. They didn't *say* it's because I was a girl, they said, 'You couldn't possibly play a tuba, it's much too big and you're much too small.' In the end, I had to choose between tenor horn, which has a really weedy little sound, and a cornet. I played that for a while, but after a year I started baritone sax and euphonium. Then one day I said to my teacher, 'I really fancy trombone.' And he gave me it right away.

NOISE-MAKERS

When schoolgirls are left alone and have the confidence to let rip, they make as much noise as the boys. Marion Fudger runs music workshops at London's Lewisham Academy of Music:

> I believe there will always be a need for all-girls' workshops. Half of those who come to me haven't tapped or hit a drum before they started because of the noise. The old 'I can't' syndrome comes out at first, but then they hear it sounding incredible and they're really thrilled – they even want to perform it!

Graduating at the age of 16 from the school brass band to Ivy Benson's All-Girl Dance Band, Annie Whitehead now runs her own quintet, is an itinerant member of several Latin and jazz bands and regularly plays guest sessions. (photo: Val Wilmer/Format)

In the North of England, for instance, they are more likely to join a brass band than an orchestra, and to learn instruments not otherwise available to them. Particularly, they are encouraged to play the cornet – a smaller, sweeter and easier-to-

At this crucial teenage time, differences in interests, confidence and aptitude separate girls and boys for ever. They listen to and appreciate pop music in completely different ways: boys talk about the music, they swap information and show off their knowledge (or pretended knowledge) about instruments and equipment; girls, on the other hand, tend to talk about the stars, looks, fashions, and the 'feel' of the song –

particularly the words and whether or not the music is good to dance to. Girls dance more than boys – and this is a key factor in the way they appreciate music – but they don't analyse it. Neither do they talk technology and equipment details. Viv Albertine's recollections sum this up:

I'd never bothered to listen to the guitar. All I was interested in was the words, the tune and the emotion. I couldn't even *hear* a guitar! And it never occurred to me that you sit for an hour before you go on stage and warm your fingers and do exercises. I used to come out of the van, hands freezing, and go and pick up the guitar, and wonder why, until the last two songs, I didn't really feel at ease with it. We didn't have the

knowledge. People don't trade it. And also, because we weren't taken seriously as musicians, they probably thought we were meant to be like that. It's not the sort of tiny detail you'd think of imparting, it's too obvious. But it's so important.'

Teen magazines like *No. 1* and *Smash Hits*, read by tens of thousands of girls, don't help, either: their interviews focus consistently on looks, occasionally on lyrics, and are fodder for more fantasies. Girls are left to find out for themselves about music, while boys trade information with each other in much the same way as they do about cars, bikes, computers, or electric guitars. The BBC TV series, *Rock School* was exceptional: shown around tea-time, just after school, it featured a drummer, a bass-player

Out of Marion Fudger's girls' music workshops came this group production of poetry, percussion, chant and dance, at the Lewisham Academy of Music's summer show, 1983. (photo: courtesy Marion Fudger)

Deirdre Cartwright, seen here on BBC TV's 'Rock School'.
(photo: courtesy Deirdre Cartwright)

know whether it's packed or spacious, but you tend not to know what the instruments are doing.

On a more personal note, I, too, can remember that same blank feeling when a musician friend tried to unscramble a record with me; to my ears, every song was 'Wall of Sound' whose elements were confusingly glued together. Now part of the pleasure of listening to music is to be able to untangle the effects, to follow an instrument through a tune, or to work out how and why a song is made. There's more to learning about pop music than conquering a handful of chords from a book.

Often women musicians learn all these things – and how to play the instruments – once the group is formed. Many individuals untangle the mysteries through workshops, which tackle jargon, technical details, as well as how songs are made up.

Such workshops for teenage girls are necessary to counter their heightened sensitivity about looks, and all the arguments against women learning instruments. Voice workshops enable women to loosen themselves and become more assertive through their voices. When Helen Terry was fed up with making a living by singing TV adverts for Hotpoint Hoovers and irons, she ran workshops for girls and young women at the Albany Empire in London. *A capella* groups such as the Mint Juleps and the Harmonettes are a new feature of the music scene which have emerged from these kinds of workshops.

YOU'RE JUST A GIRL
For women who have an irresistible fascination with horns and brass, the occupational hazards – cracked and bleeding lips, a tough ring of skin

and the electric guitarist Deirdre Cartwright demonstrating, week by week, the techniques required to play in different styles of music. The feedback was tremendous, particularly from young girls aspiring to play in a rock band; the presence of a woman playing that most hallowed of male instruments had strong reverberations.

It's much harder for girls to find a way into understanding pop music because they don't talk about it. Gina Birch of the Raincoats remembers trying to 'hear' the bass line:

I was at a friend's house when I was 18 or 19 and somebody said, 'The bass line in this is blah, blah, blah . . .' But I couldn't *hear* it. I said, 'What's the bass line?' The way I'd listened to music is how a lot of people listen – you hear a vocal, a melody, and you

A typical late '70s tale: Gina Birch (The Raincoats) bought a bass when drunk, learned to play along to favourite reggae records, and had a gig with friends three weeks later.
(photo: Shirley O'Loughlin)

across the mouth from the pressure of a mouthpiece – are cited as deterrents along with the argument about strength. Also, because wind instruments distort the face, girls are told, 'It will make you look ugly.' Annie Whitehead remembers a man coming up to her after a gig and ending his congratulations on her playing with 'It's a shame when you play because it hides your face!'

The weight argument becomes less relevant as new, lighter metals are used to make brass instruments – even with cumbersome mutes, they can be quite light. Really, though, most parents still seem to prefer their girls to learn piano or flute. Flutes are such genteel instruments, conjuring up pastoral idylls. Though used as a powerful instrument of authority by the Eurythmics' Annie Lennox, playing flute is generally seen to be like eating without letting your lips touch the food. Playing saxophone, on the other hand, is like relishing great mouthfuls of food, eating heartily for pleasure. It is a very physical involvement, and presumably this is one reason girls aren't so readily directed towards it. The saxophone has a forceful tone; even a moderately low or loud female voice coursing through the piping emerges magnified, deeper and with more presence than before. With the current revivals in rockabilly, skiffle and jazz, there are more opportunities for saxophonists in London than since the jazz heyday.

Subtler forces of discouragement are at work, too: the instruments can be heavy and awkward, which can make them difficult to learn, and require real dedication and stamina. It is now taken for granted that women can be champion swimmers or weight-lifters, and it is generally agreed that any physical exercise – be it shot-putting or ballet-dancing, drumming or guitar-playing – will equally demand body-building (maybe reshaping) and determination and training (rehearsal). But there's still a lingering suspicion about whether women can apply the required training regimes to instrument-playing, and keep up with the ardours of life on tour.

Sharon Bailey, who plays percussion with the reggae band Amazulu, claims: 'It just needs the feeling for it. You build up your strength – it's like typing: your fingers grow stronger the more you do it.'

Arguments about physical differences are usually red herrings, and they become less and less relevant as instruments become more electronic. Drum kits are now touch-sensitive: electronic syn-drums could be played by a baby with rhythm, though their being electronic sets up a new barrier to intimidate some women.

One woman who defies every argument against women's ability to play electric instruments is the legendary American session bass-player Carol Kaye. She has brought up three children and changed the sound of an instrument in pop; to this day, she remains a dedicated and disciplined player, unbelievably modest about her part in many of the classic dance-floor records of the

Carol Kaye, whose style adds melody to the rhythm function of a bass. (photo: courtesy Carol Kaye)

1960s, and film and TV soundtracks of the 1970s. She is also responsible for one of the most respected bass guitar tutors on the market. Carol started out in the jazz clubs around Los Angeles, where she worked as a guitarist and mandolin- and banjo-player. She switched to bass one day in the studio, when the session player failed to show up and his Fender bass was lying on the floor. She didn't look back.

The key to Carol Kaye's distinctive style is her use of a plectrum to pick the strings, instead of the conventional finger-plucking. 'I used the pick [plectrum] because I've played guitar since I was 13. Fingers record well, too – I have rarely used fingers and then usually only on ballads. Picking isn't as tough on the hands as finger-picking. It just builds up the thumb and right pectoris muscles.' One of the best examples of her style is the evocative, time-honoured intro to the Beach Boys' classic 'Good Vibrations'. The bass has shed its cumbersome image as a mere instrument of dull, plodding rhythms and moved across stage to join the other melody-makers. That little tune is surely one of the most familiar pop intros of all time, but Carol Kaye's bass lines also supplied the 'hooks' for most of the familiar American 1960s hit singles – from Motown (Smokey Robinson, the Supremes, Stevie Wonder) to Surf (Beach Boys, Jan and Dean), to white pop greats like Nancy Sinatra and Sonny and Cher – and even Elvis – as well as countless jazz and funk albums. In the 1970s many Hollywood soundtracks (such as the box office hit *In the Heat of the Night*) used Carol's bass to stretch tension to breaking-point.

Carol Kaye is inspiring proof against all those who argue that women can't play guitars (particularly the heavier basses) because of the instruments' weight, and because of female physiology. Nevertheless, Carol Kaye *has* suffered from over 20 years of holding that heavy plank of wood. She has now designed, for Fender, a lighter

model to save others, women *and* men, from contracting back problems like hers.

For many women the physical manifestations of their job are something to laugh – or boast – about. Speaking to Jas Obrecht of *Guitar Player*, American guitarist Nancy Wilson (Heart) laughs about the difference between her two hands, seeing in them 'the true story of my personality: one looks kind of glam, the other is a real worker hand with broken nails.' Viv Albertine recalls the *pride* the Slits felt when their fingers bled: 'When we went on tour, we played till our fingers bled, because we were so unpractised. They were nearly always in plasters – much to our great delight . . . we thought "Great, proof"!' In an interview Annie Whitehead referred to the little lump of hard skin under her bottom lip (caused by the trombone mouthpiece) as her 'little goatee' – a reference to the tufty beards some jazz musicians grow to disguise theirs.

Assuming that girls *do* cope with these arguments, assuming that they have enough determination to resist what they're taught at home and at school, how do they get into pop?

'WHOLE LOTTA PLAYIN' GOIN' ON'
The most frequent reply to my question, 'How did you come to learn a pop instrument in the first place?' involved a story about a boyfriend's guitar, or an elder brother's encouragement. Others described a well-trodden path into pop through music college, just as art college is a traditional launching-pad for many men. Such a training obviously gives them musical and technical advantages and a degree of confidence with instruments. None the less, built into the training is a masochistic sense of unattainable perfectionism and constant self-critical compari-son with 'the greats', which can be stultifying. Georgie Born (bass guitar and cello), who has always explored different areas of music, only partially completed her college course: 'It can be

just as problematic to learn the electric guitar if you are literate musically as it can be working up from scratch. The difference is that the training enables you to drop into other niches. Technique gives you entry.'

But it doesn't necessarily prepare you to play rock or pop. Carrie Booth, synth-player for the Thompson Twins:

> Generally with keyboards, you tend to get people who've come from the Royal School of Music and they know all the theory and classical techniques but they don't know how to play with feeling. I'm sure there's quite a few girl keyboard-players who can do the stuff, but they can't give it the sort of snappy feel that's needed so they don't get the jobs. There is a real difference between being able to play Beethoven and being able to join in when the band are jamming and kicking ideas around. I think women just give up too soon.

Annie Lennox of the Eurythmics studied flute and piano at the Royal College of Music. Her

She's a musician too! Annie Lennox in her other role.
(photo: Kerstin Rodgers)

ability to read music and transcribe parts gained her work at Connie Plank's illustrious Cologne Studio in Germany. What better way to learn how pop songs are structured than to have to break them apart and redistribute the parts for other musicians to play?

Studio session work is an obvious entrée into pop after music college. Ann Dudley:

> I wanted to be a session musician, but I didn't know how to go about it. I started playing electric piano and synthesizer in Mecca dance bands, and I had the advantage of being able to read [music] very well. Trevor Horn [producer of Art of Noise, Malcolm McLaren, Frankie goes to Hollywood] was in the same band, and later he more or less gave me my first session – keyboards with Dollar, then ABC and Spandau Ballet and McLaren.

She is now one of five top English producers managed by Jill Sinclair, who also runs the London SARM studios where Ann mostly works. Her string-arrangements on ABC's hit singles set a trend for increasing lushness in the sound of pop music – a deliberate reaction, perhaps, to the sparse quality of early 1980s synth music.

Another music college product, Virginia Astley, similarly drew on her training for classic arrangements within her own group, the Ravishing Beauties, and for occasional TV programme soundtracks. Her eccentric solo album, *From Gardens Where We Feel Secure*, is a dreamy excursion into an English country garden of yesteryear. Birds, insects and the village church bell accompany acoustic guitar, flute, piano and voice on the stroll. Not a late-twentieth-century instrument in earshot. But that doesn't mean classically trained musicians spurn electronics: far from it.

One distinct advantage of a classical training is the opportunity it gives players to flit from one style to another – according to taste or economic necessity. One disadvantage is the rigidity of the training, which can inhibit adaptation to the techniques of pop. Several women interviewed had gone through a self-imposed rejection of their classical training, in order to approach freely a new instrument. In complete contrast, self-taught players often develop a quirky style or personal musical sound which owes as much to their trial-and-error learning away from formal classes, as to a desire for originality. Joan Armatrading's father hid his guitar from her, so strong was his desire that she shouldn't become a musician. But she taught herself secretly. 'Initially, I didn't learn chords from a book, but just used to put my hand on the fretboard until I heard something I liked.' How much, one wonders, does her unusual guitar style – a perfect complement to her careering and swooping voice – derive from those private lessons. Many women, like Joan Armatrading, came to pop through this kind of informal improvisation.

Part of the fun of starting a group can be working out how a pop song is put together and even how to play the instruments. Viv Albertine laughs now at the thought of the Slits' early rehearsals:

Palmolive [the original drummer] was learning as much as us, but obviously, if you haven't got a solid backbeat, what chance have you got? We used to attack her mercilessly. I remember once, we were all lying around the kit, me with my foot on her foot, which was on the pedal of the bass drum, lifting it up and putting it down in time! And Ari [singer] was holding her hand ...

Sarah-Jane Owen remembers a similar Girls' Own-type scene with the Body Snatchers, before they became the Belle Stars: 'It was like the blind leading the blind. We'd all sit around an old

Dansette record-player I used on a market stall on Saturdays, and listen for the bass line ...'

'But that wasn't how you were meant to learn,' interrupted Judy Parson, the drummer. 'You were supposed to struggle in your bedroom again and again, alone, with what some guitar hero was doing, and learn to play one verse.' Boyfriends, with their freer access to instruments, can also encourage girls. Marion Fudger describes how she got into music:

At first, I was in the 'appendage-girlfriend situation' – I used to go along to my boyfriend's band's rehearsals, make the tea, and watch. I felt really excluded, they exchanged glances and smiled together, and I wished I could share that 'thing'. In those days [1969/70] you started off playing bass and as you got better you went on to rhythm guitar and then you 'arrived' at lead and played all those wanky 12-bar guitar solos. My boyfriend was making that development. One day he needed someone to play a very simple 12-bar riff on bass, so that he could jam and enjoy himself, so he taught me a 12-bar in A or E. That's when I started getting interested, but I had a horrible bass with a neck like a tree trunk that was really hard to play! We did about two gigs, then another rocky-bluesy set-up needed someone to learn loads of 12-bars over the weekend, and they asked me. Having broken away from the boyfriend's group thing, I felt more valid, but I didn't think of myself as a musician for a long time.

Judy Parsons, drummer with the Belle Stars, was also encouraged by her boyfriend:

My brother got a guitar and I thought, 'I don't want to be left out here,' so I borrowed his. I thought the Joni Mitchell image was a very nice romantic one for a woman – long hair and a guitar on your back. Looking back, that's why I think I was attracted to it – that and all my boyfriends played guitars. I definitely wanted to be in a band because it got very boring going out to see my boyfriends playing and sitting in the audience watching them. They had a much better time than I did. Then I thought of drumming – I had some bongos and I used to tap my knees a lot. I always watched the drummer because I thought that was the most interesting person in the band – not the singer. I thought it would take about two weeks to get the hang of it, but it took ages. I don't know why I carried on, I got depressed every time I tried, because I couldn't do it!

And then my boyfriend said, 'Right, you're joining this group! Come along to this gig tonight' – and he put my drums in the back of his van and shoved me on stage, and said, 'There you are!' And I played my first gig – a country and western band. I stayed with them for about a year and a half.

UP FRONT

Gradually, women are infiltrating the hallowed halls of pop and rock music. They are no longer content to accept the singular option of singing. They want to play instruments too. As more and more women appear in bands, the drum rolls and fuss which used to greet them in the past, if they were lucky – or the belittling and ridiculing which they received if they were not – begin to die down. Sufficient years have passed now for women like Carol Kaye to have made a female mark on the sound and style of their instrument. In the following brief look at the major instruments of pop music, I am most interested in the ways in which women are handling instruments, whose musical identities have matured with virtually no female involvement and whether the music they are making with them differs from that of male musicians.

KEYBOARD EXERCISES

Though the piano isn't central to either pop or rock music, it is used to add harmonic detail and embellishment. Piano was always Tin Pan Alley's accompanying instrument - as the teenaged Sandie Shaw discovered to her horror when she arrived for an audition with songwriter Tony Hatch: 'He stood there in an empty room – with just a piano.' She clammed up – before that, she'd only sung with local electric rock bands.

Pianos and female voices have long since been paired together; there is a pleasing harmonic compatibility between them, which has produced some classic blues and jazz performances. Today, the best accompaniment for the voice of both Nina Simone and Aretha Franklin remains the grand piano. Brazilian pianist Tania Maria blends her infinitely versatile voice with the lightness of electric piano, and manages to achieve a remarkable similarity of tone between them both. Her style has become increasingly percussive since she freed herself from the bland restraints of West Coast jazz-rock, and incorporated with full vigour the sambas and bossa novas which are her childhood roots.

The piano was popular among many of the singer–songwriters who reached their peak of success in the late 1960s and early 1970s. Carole King turned from writing hit songs for others (the Shirelles, Little Eva, Dusty Springfield) in New York's Brill Building, to solo work. Her album *Tapestry* sold over 13 million copies – one of the best-selling titles ever. It reveals her unique way (for the time) of matching a richly chorded piano style with a set of very personal lyrics. Joni Mitchell – possibly inspired by Carole King – started to use piano as well as acoustic guitar around 1971. Her album *Ladies of the*

Tania Maria (photo: courtesy Concord Records)

Canyon revealed a change of approach; the new songs were richer and more sophisticated, suited to the new textures of the music.

PLAY THAT BEAT

Playing a drum kit is like driving a truck – it requires good co-ordination, a fit body, good arm muscles and some physical strength – arms and feet operate separately but in harness. Drums are still very unpopular with women, though the current vogue for breaking the kit into its components has seen the appearance of women playing congas and hand-held percussion in

bands like Jeffrey Osborne's, Scritti Politti, Swann's Way, Joe Jackson's and countless others. A remaining problem is lack of role models. Even so, we have come a long way since the following story from Ginni Whitaker, drummer with the cult American protest-rock band Country Joe and the Fish, during the 1970s:

Joe called all the different agencies [in Atlanta, Georgia], and when he called mine, he said, 'Do you know any good drummers who are available?' The guy said, 'No, we don't have any drummers.' And Joe said, 'You don't have any drummers at all – no *women* drummers?' And the guy said, 'Oh, yea, wait a minute. We have one on the

Joni Mitchell: from folksy, acoustic beginnings to assured, electric maturity. (photo: Pam Isherwood/Format)

119

In 1964, Honey Lantree led her band, The Honeycombs, from the drumstool. (photo: Val Wilmer/Format)

phone.' Really, no drummers, but a woman drummer . . .

The few female drummers in the 1960s and early 1970s suffered frequent belittling and derision from their male colleagues. Journalist Val Wilmer remembers asking the Who's Keith Moon for his opinion of Honey Lantree, who drummed with the 1960s one-off hit group the Honeycombs. ' "Oh, Leadfoot Lantree, we call her," he said, dismissively. All *I* could think of was their ghastly hit record, "Have I the Right to Hold You", but inside I was thinking there must

be more than *this* for women. And yet Honey's monotonous thumping beat was no better, no worse than Dave Clark's on "Glad All Over".'

Val Wilmer's opinion about female drummers was coloured by prevailing attitudes – they simply weren't to be taken seriously. Today, 20 years later, Alannah Currie complains that people don't take her playing percussion instruments (marimbas, timbales, cowbell, etc.) seriously: 'Some people see it as *playing toys*.'

A brief craze in 1982 for 'Burundi-style' of playing – fast and furious, continuous sound, spread from an interest in African pop and ethnic music. The discovery of the stirring 'Master Drummers' from Burundi followed, influencing the charts via Adam Ant's double drum kit. At the same time King Trigger, a London group, revolved – rhythmically speaking – around Trudy Baptiste, who played a personalized, pared-down kit of snare drums. Standing behind this small unit, she used just sticks to keep up a continuous, rolling and urgent rattle with a distinctly marching quality – this later became the group's signature tune. Sandra Brown, who drummed with the all-women's punk band, the IUDs and later with Abandon your Tutu, similarly adapted her kit to her own taste: 'I hardly ever used to use hi-hat or bass drum pedal. I like to play the kit like an instrument – rather than just for rhythm.'

About 15 years earlier, the Velvet Underground's Maureen Tucker had used a minimal and idiosyncratic drum and percussion style which perfectly suited the anguished, sweet-sour romances of the group's songs: the hollow, insistent bass attack in 'Heroin', for instance, or the suspiciously sweet, music-box feel of xylophone on 'Sunday Morning'. Many years later, Maureen explained to Byron Coley in *New York Rocker* (1983) how she achieved that sinister and funereal marching drum sound:

I wanted to get an African drum sound, so I'd sit on the floor and play that. Then I got a cymbal, and I'd really play the hell out of the cymbal. After a while, our road manager built a stand to put the drums on, and then a box for the pedal so that I could use it horizontally. After that, I got a floor tom, too. I didn't get a regular kit for a long time: I don't think I was able to sit down for a couple of years, since I had to stand to play everything.

During their short careers, New York's high-on-energy-and-percussion, all-women band Pulsillama, and the cult Hispanic band ESG built brilliantly minimal pop songs out of mostly percussion heavy with Latin influences, with a few repetitive or jokey lyrics on top.

Drum kits need not be tied to the rock formulae, as those examples proved. Usually, they are restricted to a purely rhythmic function. But as Carole Kaye pointed out in *Modern Drummer* (1981): 'Drums *are* musical instru-

Josefina Cupido, a much-respected jazz drummer, whose work has ranged between theatre group (Monstrous Regiment), Lydia D'Ustebyn's Swing Orchestra, and the all-woman Latin jazz soul line-up, Guest Stars. (photo: Val Wilmer/Format)

Avoiding macho/guitar hero stances: Viv Albertine of the Slits.   (photo: David Corio)

ments. You can play songs on drums.' Though shocking to many people, this is an attitude which several female drummers and percussionists are taking to their music. In common with other instrumentalists in rock, they are not willing to be dictated to by a tradition of sweat and unsubtlety which they didn't help to create.

STRINGS ON WOOD

It's difficult to understand how a carved plank of wood, with six lengths of wound steel nailed to it and an electric current running through, came to have a gender. Electric guitars are curiously hermaphroditic. B.B. King's guitars are all called 'Lucille', after his hit song. Angus Young of the heavy metal band AC/DC once fantasized in *Rolling Stone* about his ideal guitar, speaking no doubt for many players: 'My fantasy would be a cannon that shot sperm at the audience.' The instrument became utterly male-identified within 1960s rock music. Jimi Hendrix alternately performed oral sex and masturbated with his machines, while the Clash used guitars as both phallus and gun. Mostly, though, they are treated like female bodies, except when female bodies are being used to sell them – then, suddenly, they become phallic. Recently, bands like the Smiths have retrieved a delicate jangley sound from the psychedelic era, and there are encouraging signs that many male musicians are effectively finding ways of dispensing with rock's dominating solos.

Charlotte Caffey, of the Go-Gos, also creates a light, luminous quality (and some heavy rock, too). Nevertheless, plenty of women still conform to a swirling, classic rock style which dictates the way the guitar sounds *and* how it is played. In certain kinds of music – jazz and blues, especially – guitarists play seated; the obligatory pose for a rock musician on the other hand, is a standing pose, a strut and thrust. Viv Albertine describes the insidious infectiousness of this stance:

It was difficult to move with the guitar without strutting, at first. When I was learning how to stand up and play at the same time, I stood with my legs apart quite a lot. But I honestly think that most guitarists do it for balance, especially when you're not good. It's hard looking at the guitar, holding it, playing it *and* singing.

Viv's guitar used to look like an accessory, slung like a scarf round her neck; she completely overcame any of its machoness, didn't solo, and kept to a tuneful rhythm function.

On the point about standing versus sitting more generally: reed-player Lindsay Cooper found standing up to play a relief – and, further – it made her feel more powerful and confident after years of sitting:

Since Henry Cow, I've never sat down for a gig – except with the Mike Westbrook Band, where we *all* sit. I found it particularly liberating ... for a woman to stand up. You become really aware of your presence on stage, whereas if you're sitting, it feeds into the idea that you're not very important. As soon as I started to stand up, I realized what a terrible restriction it had been, and I think it did slow down the process of feeling confident on stage, and of being in charge of yourself, and able to move around.

The electric guitar has become the most fetishized object in Western pop music: for a long time, Viv Albertine wouldn't discuss guitars – even though she collected them for their very different sounds and functions; she refused to play in a guitar festival because she loathed the idea of separating the instrument off and making it special.

In many kinds of African pop music, there is no

parallel to the rigid hierarchy of rock, with 'lead' guitar at the top. Solos – in any case, infrequent – carry equal status regardless of the instrument. Several guitarists tend to work together to create a shifting, undulating block of sound. Vicki Aspinall has studied African guitar style for some time:

> I find it interesting that some of the things I've been learning seem to be similar to the way I was playing in the Raincoats. Not knowing the standard chord progressions, and many of the rock tricks on the guitar, and not learning through, say, folk guitar, I had to invent ways of playing it. And I found that those connected up with some of the rhythm playing in the African style (actually, the Zaïrois style, *soukous*) – obvious things like using just three strings instead of all six, playing the top part of a chord on the bottom part of the string, picking out little figures and using them repeatedly, and playing a fairly asymmetrical pattern that starts and stops, and starts again, without taking any notice of the bar lines ... which is what we did in the Raincoats anyway.

When women pick up guitars they don't pick up the weight of a generation or two of guitar heroes associated with them. The chances are they haven't singled out 'great guitar solos' to drool over and copy note by note. Guitarists in women's rock bands in the 1970s, and countless individuals since, have down-graded the instrument and broken with rock's tradition of awesome, conversation-stopping solos. There is no new style, as such, just a change of status that gives rise to some optimism about the future – especially as the revision of old, worn-out formulae is now making itself felt among male guitarists, too.

ACOUSTIC FLAVOURS

The most frequently trodden path to playing electric guitar is through folk, acoustic instruments. Joan Baez's 1959 appearance at the Newport Folk Festival set a trend for women singing political lyrics and playing acoustic guitar. In country music, the instrument was always *the* partner for most singers – from Dolly Parton to Emmylou Harris, both fine players.

Probably because of its associations with both folk music *and* women, the acoustic guitar is not highly rated by the snobbish rock world. It is, however, beginning to make a come-back as an occasional source of fresh, light textures in some arrangements. Strawberry Switchblade are two young Glaswegian women whose anachronistic visual style (polka dots, heavy black eyeliner, stilettoes) complements their unsophisticated, unselfconscious adoption of folky pop; simple, sad melodies; wistful, reflective lyrics; an accompaniment of simple, folk-club acoustic guitar chords. The effect is a curiously appealing *déja vu* – as though a folk- or skiffle-club duo have been transported into the 1980s and, like guileless ingenues, wonder at the bewilderment they evoke.

BASS LINES

The instrument with greatest appeal to women during the rush to form punk bands was undoubtedly the electric bass. With only four strings against the guitar's six, it was assumed to be (and is) easier to play. It is not played chordally, so single notes are easy to find, to thread behind a tune. It's an instrument that's quicker to yield some results, and that speed makes for confidence. In almost all kinds of popular and dance music, the bass forms an anchor, working with the drums, in shapes built

Vicki Aspinall's classical training as a skilled violinist introduced a novel flavour to the Raincoats' music. (photo: Santo Basone)

from a set of short, repeated patterns.

The reasons for its popularity with women remain obscure. There is certainly a tremendous sense of physical power and pleasure to be gained from plucking those thick steel strings which reverberate through your stomach. Georgie Born suggests that the way a bass is tuned for rock is ideally suited to a smaller woman's hand – the shapes of the rhythm part lie under the thumb and fingers within easy reach.

Reggae's overriding influence in the 1970s must have been partly responsible for the focus to fall on the bass. It is so central to reggae, and so tuneful – it also sounds misleadingly simple. Reggae rhythms were often the basis of songs by mixed or women's bands – the Slits, Mistakes, Au Pairs, Tour de Force, Mo-Dettes, Talking Heads, Raincoats, and so on.

The bass came to the fore in funk and dance music in the late 1970s; in soul music, it had always been crucial. There are some well-respected female players in American dance music – Kim Clarke (ex-Defunkt) now leads her own, all-women funk band in New York; Carol Kaye, who began as a jazz guitarist, made the natural progression from 1960s pop into jazz-funk in the 1970s: versatile Carol Colman contributes a jaunty, Latin jazz or funk touch to Kid Creole's music.

In the 1960s, *Downbeat* magazine described Carol Kaye as 'a chick with a pick'. Today, there are so many – and so many *good* – female bass-players, that they no longer elicit special mention on grounds of their gender. The same cannot yet be said in relation to any other rock or pop instrument.

TECHNO-ELECTRO GENERATION

In 1968, a young New York singer, songwriter and keyboards-player was given one of the first synthesizers by its inventor, Robert Moog. Annette Peacock used that machine to 'treat' her voice, so starting a practice common in most recording studios today. Nearly 20 years later, another New Yorker – Laurie Anderson – presents a complex audio-visual show via a combination of electronics, pre-recorded tapes, a vocoder (to disguise her voice) and various inventions of her own. Unlike Laurie Anderson, Annette Peacock never managed to bridge avant-garde and pop. She remains (working now in England) in the respected ranks behind the stars, where usually some of the most imaginative experiments are made. It is only later that popularizers like Laurie Anderson might make them available to the mainstream.

The music scene in England doesn't emulate New York's easy integration between the two camps illustrated by the careers of both Nona Hendryx and Adele Bertei: singers who fuse rock and dance music, with the possibilities of electronics and effects, while basically aiming for a mainstream, chart market. Laurie Anderson seems to have stumbled on chart success (with the single 'Oh Superman'). Most of her original inspiration is traceable to the 1960s organization Fluxus. Fluxus members made their own instruments, mixed their media, treated their environment as a source of usable sound, and generally sowed the seeds of ideas which are the currency of contemporary videos, art-rock performances and musical styles. Yoko Ono, as part of Fluxus, reached into the commercial market through her recordings with the Plastic Ono Band and John Lennon's reputation. Though Ono's voice was 'untreated' (in the sense of Laurie Anderson's) the startling and perfectly evocative effects she achieved were similar to those made today with the help of synthesizers. Both style and intention are directly comparable: the conversion of the voice into another instrument; its employment as a source of 'white noise'. Laurie Anderson's homemade instruments – her 'talking' violin, for instance – have the advantage of micro-techno-

Laurie Anderson, 1982.   (photo: Pam Isherwood/Format)

logy. The strings are replaced by a tape-head receiver, and, instead of horsehairs, the bow is strung with a pre-recorded tape which plays as the bow makes contact. Her skill and presence in performance is quite exceptional. Small, neat and very methodical in every movement and gesture, Laurie Anderson is more evocative of *Tomorrow's World* than the world of rock.

Seeing Laurie Anderson perform in England is still an inspiring experience even though much of the content is pretentious and boring. Synthesizers and electronics are still very much boys' toys in the UK – though there are signs of change. During the synth-band boom of the early 1980s, the Monochrome Set and a handful of lesser-known bands contained women members. One of the most anonymous female players has to be Gillian Gilbert who, as part of the unprecedentedly low-profile New Order, provided the swirling synthesizers to the band's hit single, 'Blue Monday' (at the time, Britain's best-selling 12" ever).

Let's end with a word of advice to budding female synth-players. It comes from Carrie Booth, formerly with the Monochrome Set and now with the Thompson Twins: 'The technical side does tend to put women off. More men get into that stuff. I found it hard, because I'd much rather spend time getting a riff together than finding out about how computers work. But it's something you've *got* to do.'

A JAZZ, JITTER AND JIVE EXCURSION

Some female musicians, influenced by feminism, consciously elect to work 'outside', the mainstream and see forming all-women bands as a way of making a political statement. The aim is a determinedly un-aggressive, non-hierarchical music, created within a non-competitive, sisterly climate. Through a feminist analysis, rock music is singled out as being essentially male, and 'cock rock' the most explicit and crude expression of male sexuality: loud and obtrusive, built out of a series of peaks and wanings, in a performance which is a series of sexual simulations and associations, aimed at a predominantly male audience.

Women's ability to enjoy themselves and each other without relying on the presence – and the promise – of men, was what made women-only gigs an obvious new venture in the mid-1970s. They can create a warm and exciting atmosphere between audience and performer, less to do with the leery voyeurism that women performers in front of men are frequently subjected to.

Even before the current feminism, women-only bands were a feature of the musical landscape – considered a bit weird maybe, having to be twice as good, certainly, but there all the same. At the turn of the century, ladies' orchestras played tea dances, parties and bazaars (fondly recalled in Greta Kent's book *A View from the Bandstand*). Ivy Benson put together *her* first band, playing the pop songs of their day, in late 1930s. Their big break came during the war, when Mecca dance halls first recruited women. After 1945, they had fewer problems: Ivy had a guaranteed audience of troops who were by then based in Germany and wanted to see familiar faces.

Undeniably, Ivy Benson's band was a crucial outlet for talented women who had a passion for popular music, but nowhere to play it. Some came straight from school, many needed Ivy's personal tuition to gain full proficiency on their instrument. Sheila Tracey, for example, had graduated from the Royal College of Music in the 1950s on trombone and piano. Anxious not to fall into the teaching trap, she asked Ivy for a job. 'I'd never learned jazz on the trombone: I'd

Gillian Gilbert is one of the very few women synthesizer players in Britain. Mostly because of the group's fervent anti-publicity attitude, Gillian remains largely unknown for her part in the music of New Order. (photo: Peter Anderson)

Ivy Benson's All-Girl Dance Band in their '50s heyday. Ivy,
performer/bandleader, has devoted her musical life to training
and encouraging young women musicians.
(photo: courtesy of Sheila Tracy – trombonist, far right of picture)

never played off-the-beat or "anticipation", which is used all the time in jazz. I learned all I had to know about dance music from Ivy Benson.' Twenty years later, another trombonist – Annie Whitehead – left home and school behind in Oldham, and went on the road to Germany with Ivy Benson's band. A veteran of the school brass band and local dance bands, she was undaunted by the pile of sheet music which confronted every player. It was essential for all members to be able to read music; every tune was written out, including the solos. Ivy says she never learned to improvise herself, and that 'Very few of the girls could – they weren't allowed in jazz bands, so how could they learn?' Ivy's musical straitjacket never fitted Annie Whitehead too well; the first time she nipped off after a gig with some friends for a 'free blow', Ivy walked in on her. The next night, Annie had to pay the price for her musical treachery: 'Suddenly Ivy thrust an arrangement at me and I had to be the star of the show and play all the solos, note perfect!'

By all accounts, Ivy Benson ran her band like a cross between St Trinians and a woman's army camp. She told her girls what to wear, what to play and where – and where not – to go. If badly riled she would stand with her back to the audience and utter the ultimate insult: 'I wish I was in front of a man's band . . . ' But she never was. Not in 40 years. She chose to work only with women because she believed they should be given the opportunity to play. It wasn't a gimmick (though it was sometimes treated like one); it didn't even work to their advantage like it might today. The women's bands were a practical solution to a male closed shop which operated in almost all of the big-name Big Bands regardless of the talent of the female musician. All-women line-ups were an obvious pragmatic alternative.

Todays' blurring of boundaries between jazz, show business and dance music has led to a renewed interest in the kind of music Ivy Benson used to play, 30 years ago, though the bands are now less regimented and the music less orchestrated. Jazz has become fashionable again. Singer Alison Stratton moved from the poppy Young Marble Giants to the more Latin jazz-orientated Weekend; Tracey Thorn switched from the Marine Girls' deadpan attempts at samba-style to the more ambitious and polished arrangements of Weekend's successor, Working Week. Neneh Cherry sang with the proto pop–jazz group Rip Rig and Panic, and neo-torch singers Carmel and Sade have recently brought their blues and jazz versions into the charts. Sambas and Latin jazz are the order of the day; saxophones and horns are essential instruments once more. This has brought a sprinkling of welcome female faces behind the mouthpieces – though not always for the best reasons: it was noticeable that the Style Council used two young women miming on *Top of the Pops*, but not *playing* live on tour.

The women's jazz and soul scene, small though it is in comparison to the chart-makers, thrives through a well-established, and well-attended network of courses and workshops. Another factor is the number of bands, which are constantly reforming and changing around a steady core of professional and talented musicians . . . Lydia D'Ustebyn's Swing Orchestra, the Guest Stars, the Holloway All-Stars (mixed), Harmonettes, Toot Sweet, Hipscats, Hi-Jinx, and the legendary big band Sisterhood of Spit. Sisterhood of Spit (SoS) was a 20-plus piece band, whose reputation exceeded their number of performances (they made one recording –the *Making Waves* compilation). It was, however, a valuable learning process for a fleet of skilful players who subsequently emerged on the scene, to form their own, more modest (in size) line-ups. From SoS, they had acquired confidence and skill. A most important feature of SoS was its collectivity and emphatic disregard for the mystiques and relative status of instruments.

Equally significant was their promotion of improvisation as a skill to be encouraged rather than feared. The Feminist Improvising Group (FIG) based themselves totally on the quicksands of improvisation – in both music *and* performance. Like SoS, they were a fluctuating group, whose skills and musical experiences were as varied as their ages and tastes. The pool included players from Holland, Switzerland and England; their stylistic range encompassed free jazz, performance art, women's music (Ova) and experimental rock (Henry Cow). The nature of an event would reflect this diversity: it could be a series of loosely planned satirical sketches, with flashes of musical accompaniment; it might, just as easily, turn out to be a full set of improvisations drawing on myriad sounds, tunes and moods. The act was always connected with the roles and expectations for women within different kinds of music – rock, jazz or classical – and, as such, was uniquely analytical. Although in no way a rock band (despite producing pertinent and astute pop parodies), FIG built up a solid following in Britain and, especially, in Europe where the barriers between jazz and rock are less rigid and exclusive. Their greatest impact was on the women in the audience. Lindsay Cooper looks back on that time: 'We were part of the general

The short-lived Sisterhood of Spit, rehearsing vocals.   (photo: Val Wilmer/Format)

Ova: England's most prolific and active feminist musicians, who draw on women's folk music from around the world.
(photo: Anna Arnone)

broadening of women's musical horizons and the feedback was terribly exhilarating.' Their ability to take risks, musically and in performance, put them as close to the experimental punk line (exemplified at that time by the Raincoats) as to the avant-garde. FIG folded in 1981; but even their couple of years' existence had caused many people to question how they respond to, and what they expect from, what they see on stage.

In a period of musical fluidity and cross-over, it became possible for women to learn and play instruments that had previously been seen as male prerogatives.

ALL-GIRL BANDS

In 1974, Nona Hendryx's then group, LaBelle, sang 'All-Girl Band', 'dealing with the facts and the pain' of being on the road, away from home and loved ones. All-girl groups had been proliferating in America for some time – with Fanny, Isis, Birtha, Pride of Women. But when manager Kim Fowley just took on the Runaways that year he set out to manipulate them into a money-spinning gimmick. Many women don't support women-only line-ups because they won't be taken seriously. Carol Colman had particularly strong feelings on this: 'All-female groups are a man's concept,' she insisted.

They were originally put together by male

producers to make money. They might as well be go-go girls or strippers – there is that kind of sensationalism around an all-female band. Once you get boxed into that kind of position, a stigma becomes attached to you. You are not taken seriously. You are spoken of as a woman who plays well – or, as they say in New York, "She plays great for a woman." Social pressures force you to go outside society to seek a way to survive. But I say, 'Stay in! Stay in the community! Get your position. Why be banished?'

Carol Colman's talent and reputation make it easier for her to say this now; less confident women are still at the mercy of the traditional attitudes to them as musicians, as Carrie Booth explained:

When you're in a band with all blokes they either treat you very special and nicely, or else they so much don't want to make exceptions that they in fact treat you terribly . . . When you're on tour, when it suits them, you're one of the lads, when it doesn't, you're not. In one band, when they went out hunting women, they wouldn't want me along; but when it came to mucking in with the gear and helping load the van, they wouldn't do it for me because I was supposed to be one of the gang!

Afrikan Woman (Mwanamke Mwafrika) performing at the Women Live International Day, in London;
a roots reggae sound from an all-woman band.   (photo: Pam Isherwood/Format)

135

A NEW TRADITION

Carol Kaye is a legend in her own lifetime, though mainly as a musician's musician. However, Carol Colman (bass-player with Kid Creole and the Coconuts) spoke about her during our interview, and revealed a knowledgeable and professional reverence for her. A sense of female lineage is emerging: women musicians generally are very aware of how others are playing, and who's on the scene. Conversation with the Belle Stars turned to instruments, and the quirky techniques some women use. Apart from their interesting observations, it was an example of hearing women talk to each other – positively, seriously, eagerly – about each other *as musicians*.

Sarah-Jane Owen: I was thinking about Tina Weymouth [Talking Heads] – she's got this odd way of playing, plucking with her right thumb, which is probably a habit she got into when she couldn't get these two fingers to do it.

Clare Hurst: And Kim Clarke [ex-Defunkt] has got this really weird style of playing. Maybe it's because of her big hands and enormously long fingers.

Sarah-Jane: I'm sure it's being confronted with your instrument and thinking, 'God, how do they get their hands round that?' and then developing your own way of doing it. Maybe she was a guitarist, because when I get hold of a bass, I use my thumb a bit, from holding the pick. I find it quite easy to pluck with my thumb, and it's easy to develop different styles.

'Guesting' on other people's live shows and records is taken very much for granted in all kinds of pop music. It is possible to track musicians from one milestone album on, say, the soul circuit, to another. It's no big deal – it's part of the process of change in music, and a healthy creative fusion. But even at superstar level, this musical chairs is largely a male game in the studios. For live gigs it adds a certain kudos to use women. Nevertheless, apart from notable exceptions like Joe Jackson, who seems to go out of his way to use women in all his work, the examples are rare enough for to make you nudge your neighbour.

When Vicki Wickham was working on Nona Hendryx's 1983 solo album, *On One Track, Design for Living*, 'Nona used all women musicians. She had Gina Shock (drummer with the Go-Gos), Tina Weymouth (Talking Heads), Valerie Simpson (pianist, singer, song-writer of the Ashford-Simpson Band), Nancy Wilson (guitarist with Heart), Laurie Anderson on violin, and Patti LaBelle did back-up vocals. All of them said they'd never been asked before to play on anyone else's album. These are all accomplished, great musicians, in groups that are really well-known.'

Such a session would have been inconceivable as little as 20 years ago. A determined producer *might* have managed to bring together female musicians to fill the chairs, because, as this book has stressed all the way through, women have always played every kind of instrument, regardless of the social taboos attached. The major change in the last decade has been a numerical one. Carol Kaye explained – rather regretfully – that when she started playing in the 50s: 'I was just about the only woman on the West Coast jazz scene – and a white woman at that. There weren't any role models then to encourage others to play.'

Sandie Shaw couldn't remember *any* female musicians in her 1960s heyday – but that is partly a fault of 'public memory'; there *were* women, but their numbers were so slight and their significance so neglected that the individuals have been forgotten – except for ridicule, like 'Leadfoot Lantree'.

The mushrooming began in earnest in the

1970s. Today we are seeing the effects of women performers inspiring and encouraging others, of an efficient workshop circuit for novices and unconfident beginners, and an industry with more women than ever before in positions of power, able to give others a chance. But there is still the mass aversion or resistance or fear of certain instruments, particularly drums and electric guitars, in this country. Otherwise, it is impossible not to feel tremendous optimism about the future role women will play in shaping the sound of pop music – and more subtly, on the ways women in groups organise and present it.

A member of Three Tons of Joy (predecessor to Two Tons of Fun) with '50s bandleader Johnny Otis. (photo: courtesy Charlie Gillett)

CHAPTER SEVEN

ALL OF YOU

SHERYL GARRATT

Just one touch: a fan proudly wears Keith Richard's autograph on her cheek, 1965.
(photo: Val Wilmer/Format)

TEENAGE DREAMS

It's a teenage dream to be seventeen
And to find you're all wrapped up in love.
— 'Give A Little Love', the Bay City Rollers

One of my clearest memories from nine years ago is of a bus ride from my housing estate in Birmingham into the city centre. An atmosphere like a cup final coach, but with all of us on the same side and with one even more radical difference – there were no boys. At every stop, more and more girls got on, laughing, shouting, singing the songs we all knew off by heart. We compared the outfits and banners we had spent hours making, swapped jokes and stories, and talked happily to complete strangers because we all had an interest in common: we were about to see the Bay City Rollers.

That was 5 May 1975. I know the exact date because the ticket stub was carefully preserved in my scrapbooks, along with every one of that year's press-cuttings to refer to the Rollers. And they were mentioned a lot. Tartan was the year's most fashionable accessory; you could buy Bay City socks, knickers, watches, shoes, lampshades and countless other fetish objects to fantasize over. For a while at least, the Rollers were big business. Yet nine years on, I see that they didn't even play on their early records; the songs that reached the Top Ten on advance orders alone were weak and sloppily made, with words so wet they almost dripped off the vinyl. Considering that we were supposedly driven into a frenzy the second they walked on stage, they weren't even that pretty.

So what *was* the appeal? Johnny Ray, Sinatra, Billy Fury, Cliff Richard, the Beatles, Bolan, the Osmonds, Duran Duran, Nik Kershaw . . . the names have changed, the process of capitalizing on the phenomenon may have become more efficient and calculated, but from my mother to my younger cousin, most women go through

'that phase'. Most of us scream ourselves silly at a concert at least once, although many refuse to admit it later, because like a lot of female experience, our teen infatuations have been trivialized, dismissed and so silenced. Wetting

Power and pleasure: Wham! fans, 1983.   (photo: Kerstin Rodgers)

your knickers over a pop group just isn't a 'hip' thing to have done – much better to pretend you spent your formative years listening to Northern Soul or Billie Holiday.

Even the artists making money out of girls' fantasies are usually embarrassed and at pains to point out that they have *male* fans, too: to get out of the teeny trap and aim their music at a more 'mature' or serious audience seems to be their general ambition. Once they've attained those heights, they're quick to sneer at the girls who helped make them in the first place. Of course, the serious, thinking rock audience they want is mainly male. Only 28 per cent of NME's readership are women, for instance, as opposed to an estimated 40 per cent for the younger, glossier, less analytical *Smash Hits*. In spite of a number of women journalists (and some men who make the effort), the music press is mainly written by men for other men. 'Primarily for men' is a message that permeates the ads and the way they use women's bodies to shift product, and that informs the casual sexism of articles on women artists (the references to 'dogs' and 'boilers' in *Sounds*, for example). As part of the same bias, 'teenybop' music is either ignored or made into a joke. Often with justice, of course: the Rollers may have been atrocious, but later bands have plumbed depths that my little Scots boys couldn't have dreamed of.

But no matter how bad the music, what the press or any of the self-appointed analysts of 'popular culture' fail to reflect is that the whole pop structure rests on the backs of these 'silly, screaming girls'. They bought the records in millions and made a massive contribution to the early success of Elvis, the Beatles, the Stones, Marc Bolan, Michael Jackson and many of the others who have since been accepted by the grown-ups and become monuments, reference-points in the rock hierarchy. Before you sneer again, boys, remember that it's often their money that allows you your pretensions.

But the real question is, of course, why? Why do adolescent girls go loopy over gawky, sometimes talentless young men? The answer lies partly in the whole situation of adolescent women in our society. We live in a world where sex has become a commodity – used to sell everything from chocolate to cars, sold in films and magazines, and shown everywhere to be a wonderful, desirable ideal that is central to our lives. The pages of *Jackie*, *My Guy* and countless others, have a clear message: look good, shape up and flaunt it. Yet hand in glove with this dictum there goes another: *nice girls don't do it* – or at least not until they're 16/ married/ going steady (and, even then, they don't take the initiative). Sex is the sweetest con-trick of our time, a candy-coated sweetie with a guilt-filled centre. At adolescence, we start to realize that this magic/punishment may actually apply to us, too.

A confusing and often traumatic time for everyone. For girls, however, these new expectations, the new rules and roles they have to conform to, are even more perplexing. Growing aware of our bodies and needs is alarming, because while male sexuality is exaggerated by society – portrayed as insatiable and uncontrollable – ours has been virtually obliterated. It is men who *need* sex; women supply it (though it is our responsibility to keep him at bay until the time is right). With double standards, feelings we aren't supposed to *have* – let alone enjoy – and a body or ambitions that may not fit the acceptable stereotypes, it can be a pretty tough time. Falling in love with posters can be a way of excluding real males and of hanging on to that ideal of 'true love' for just a little longer. It is a safe focus for all that newly discovered sexual energy, and a scream can often be its only release. It is the sound of young women, not 'hysterical schoolgirls' as one reporter would have it – a scream of defiance, celebration, and excitement.

'When their fans are old enough to start looking for *real* boyfriends,' sneered a *Birmingham Evening Mail* review of that May 1975 show, the Rollers will soon be forgotten.' But it's not that simple: some of us were lesbians, some of us *did* have boyfriends. In any case, girls mature earlier than boys, so it was more a question of us waiting for *them* to grow up than the other way round.

R 'n b singer LaVern Baker around 1965, meeting her fans to promote one of her many hit singles.
(photo: courtesy Charlie Gillett)

.Carol Bedford, who wrote *Waiting for the Beatles* about her experiences as an avid Beatles follower, firmly dismissed the idea that their obsession was due to any fear of sex. In an interview in the *News of the World's* Sunday magazine (5 April 1984), she says:

We weren't neurotic and we weren't all virgins. I knew what sex was, I'd lived with a man – so it can't be true. And I didn't get afraid or hysterical when George [Harrison, her favourite] did touch me. I didn't want to go further because if he did have a 'stable', I didn't want to be one of a crowd. Of course, it must have been an escape from reality into an idealized relationship. But that's wonderful and I wish I had an escape now. I knew what was important then – seeing George. Today, I couldn't answer that. I keep in touch with the other Scruffs [the name adopted by the gang of women who sat outside the band's offices all day]. We remember it as a giggling and happy time. Life is much harder now.

Part of the appeal is desire for comradeship. With the Rollers at least, many became involved not because they particularly liked the music, but because they didn't want to miss out. We were a gang of girls having fun together, able to identify each other by tartan scarves and badges. Women are in the minority on demonstrations, in union meetings, or in the crowd at football matches: at the concerts, many were experiencing mass power for the first and last time. Looking back now, I hardly remember the gigs themselves, the songs, or even what the Rollers looked like. What I *do* remember are the bus rides, running home from school together to get to someone's house in time to watch *Shang-A-Lang* on TV, dancing in lines at the school disco and sitting in each others' bedrooms discussing our fantasies and compiling our scrapbooks. Our real obsession was with ourselves; in the end, the actual men behind the posters had very little to do with it at all.

But why those particular men? It is interesting to note that although many of their lyrics tell how girls continually lust over their irresistible bodies, Rainbow, Whitesnake, or even the more enlightened, younger heavy metal bands just don't get women screaming at them. The people most attracted to the ideal of the hard, hairy, virile hunk of male are, in fact, other men, who form the majority of the audience at any heavy metal gig. Women seem far more excited by slim, unthreatening, baby-faced types who act vulnerable and who resemble them. Androgyny is what they want: men they can dress like and identify with, as well as drool over. With so few women performers to use as models, perhaps girlish boys are the next best thing. There's no way you could imitate Whitesnake's David Coverdale; a Rollers

loo-brush haircut or a Brian Jones pageboy, on the other hand, was easy. Furthermore, you, too, could wear the same clothes as those slim-hipped, pretty young boys. It is easy to forget that even the Rolling Stones - now Real Men without question - were once condemned for their effeminacy and implied to be gay.

A touch of homosexuality seems to *enhance* a male star's popularity with women, in fact - especially if it is carefully denied elsewhere. When Marc Bolan' ex-manager, Simon Napier-Bell, took on Wham! after seeing them on *Top of the Pops*, he knew that their exclusive, buddy-boy act would go down as well with a young female audience as it had with the clientele of Bolts, a North London gay club. Many stars are openly bisexual, knowing that it adds to their infamy and appeal. Even Frankie Goes to Hollywood - whose first record was banned from the BBC due to its gay overtones - found they had attracted a teeny audience. This success caused them to consider toning down their act, they said in the gay magazine *Square Peg*:

> I think we are paddling backwards, because we've realized that there's a lot of money to be made out of 13-year-old girls, which is sad. But we've been told by people in office buildings that we're treading on thin ice now, to be careful - not that we're going to be that careful. I'm not singing for 13-year-olds, I'm still singing for men.

Roxy Music, Bowie, Bolan, The Sweet, Adam Ant and Boy George have all used camp presentation to advantage; one of the Bay City Rollers had formerly posed for gay porn magazines (which, of course, says more about his financial state than his sexuality). Even cuddly Barry Manilow, the aural equivalent of Mills and Boon, began his career playing the gay clubs with Bette Midler. This isn't to say that all of the people mentioned here *are* gay - but the notion that they *may* be somehow enhances their appeal to women. Perhaps it makes them safer? Or perhaps this hint of deviancy titillates. Maybe even women feel that they would be the one to mother the boy, to love him and set him back on the right path.

The idea of the hero as an outsider is very important. After all, young women are having problems adapting to that same alienating society themselves. This 'bad boy' image has been a powerful theme for pop heroes. It links together groups like the Stones and early Wham! – otherwise very far apart. These boys are the ones your parents definitely wouldn't like – nor, for that matter, would your straight and prissy classmates. They, like you, don't fit in. But they're rebels not rejects, and by liking them, you too become a rebel.

A lifetime of suppression means that few girls dream of themselves becoming exceptional: instead, they fantasize about having boyfriends who do it for them, projecting their desires yet again on to men. With songs such as 'He's a Rebel', 'Home of the Brave' and, of course, 'Leader of the Pack', the Crystals and the Shangri-Las built careers around the contradictions that male stars often pander to. Rebels by proxy, girls envied for their associations with wild men, they were still ultimately safe, took mom's advice, and snuggled sadly back into the family fold.

Most groups choose a safer path, and are at pains to present a reassuringly wholesome image for parents and the media. Girls' magazines are usually happy to help, as in this conversation overheard in a record company office:

Reporter: What do you eat for breakfast?
Singer: Fried eggs, bacon, beans and tea.
Reporter: Isn't that a bit lumpen?
Singer: How about champagne and kippers, then?
Reporter: A little too exotic, I think.
Singer: OK. Coffee, toast, and marmalade?
Reporter: Great. What's your favourite drink?

And a thousand 12-year-olds cut it out and put it in their scrapbooks, knowing they'll be able to cook him what he wants when he comes to stay.

Even with the sickeningly wholesome Osmonds or the Rollers, however, the feeling of going against normal society, of rebellion, persisted. One of the most important points about most teeny groups is that almost everyone else hates them. With the Rollers, everyone but the fans continually made fun of us, insisting that the band looked stupid and couldn't play. They were right, of course, but that wasn't the point. It was us against the world – and, for a while at least, we were winning.

For the girls' magazines, the band meant big circulation. When guitarist Alan Longmuir tried to escape from the band pleading old age (probably yet another publicity stunt), many even printed petition forms. Presumably in exchange for the endless colour posters and the fawning coverage they gave the band, *Mirabelle* and *Fab 208* were allowed to print weekly 'letters' from the boys. I hardly missed a copy. The few brave souls who did dare to criticize were usually forced to retract due to the sheer volume of abuse; next to each of these apologies, I lovingly drew a little skull-and-crossbones victory sign. We were invincible, a tartan army defying critics, DJs, papers and everyone else who spoke against 'our boys'.

In the end, media attention was so focused on the fans and the mass hysteria that the music itself was forgotten altogether. The Rollers were accused of engineering their first US TV appearance so that fans surged forward and knocked two of them unconscious minutes into their act. The estimated 50 million viewers of the satellite broadcast didn't get to *hear* much, but they saw what manager Tam Paton wanted them to see: Rollermania. It meant that when they made their first visit to the USA a week later, there were already tartan hordes waiting at the airport,

The girls room, 1984. A private space plot, to preen, and to exchange stories: is she really going out with him?
(photo: Kerstin Rodgers)

ready to join the fun. It takes an efficient publicity machine to escalate one single teeny band into a mass phenomenon, and Tam Paton was a slick manipulator of the media and pop. As he trumpeted in a *Daily Mirror* piece:

> I used to pick Rollers on personality rather than on skill. I felt you could take someone who had an image and teach him to play. You can have the most fantastic musician in the world, but what's the point if you have to spend a fortune in plastic surgery to get him right as far as image is concerned?

The ultimate in this selection process is perhaps the New York/ Puerto Rican Group, Menudo, whose members have to be under 16, and good looking. They are unceremoniously sacked on their sixteenth birthday, and replaced.

It is looks that attract the magazines that tell young women how to look and what to buy. 'Personality' is what these magazines promote: they will interview stars about food, pets, or (clean) funny stories about life on the road. They are not interested in music: how or what the artists play – lyrics aside – is usually irrelevant; even the inevitable colour posters rarely show the band actually performing. What girls are sold is a catchy hook, and an image and lyrics they can identify with. Fantasy fodder. This is the male as sex object, posed, airbrushed and marketed just like any female model. He, however, is usually imperfect and ordinary enough for the fans to believe that, one day, he could be theirs.

That myth, the illusion of accessibility, is essential – and artists aiming for this market are careful never to mention a girlfriend or even the type of woman they prefer in any but the vaguest terms. Once again, the Rollers had the routine down to perfection: 'It's not looks that count, it's personality,' said Les McKeowan, giving hope to plain girls everywhere, while forgetting to mention his friendships with women like Britt Ekland.

A fan's mind is a curious thing, though. It picks and chooses from the information available, giving credence only where it wants to, and even managing to retain and believe quite contradictory facts simultaneously. Fantasy, unlike reality, isn't binding, which is the big advantage pop heroes have over real men. You can turn Boy George into your gentle, cuddly, funny, dream romance and still enjoy watching your father turning purple with anger over his effeminacy.

In every interview there's an endless litany of 'no permanent girl at the moment . . . some day I'll find the right girl . . . believe in romance . . . we love all our fans.' You know it's you he's really waiting for. But you also know he's unavailable. And there's the crunch. Normally, even the most obsessive fan knows that her chances are so slight as to be negligible. Jona MacDonald first saw Chris Hughes on *Top of the Pops*, in 1979, drumming with Adam and the Ants. She went on to follow him with an energy, persistence and ingenuity that begs admiration in spite of its being so pointless and oppressive. In 1983, she sat on the steps of the Abbey Road Studios morning and night for a total of 110 days (she counted), while he produced Wang Chung's first album, *Points on a Curve*. Years before, Beatles fan Jill Pitchard had waited outside those same studios for so long that she was eventually made

the receptionist: she is still there, and when EMI opened the room in which the Beatles recorded to the public, Jona was offered a job alongside Jill, ushering in awestruck fans.

So what's the appeal of famous men?

I don't look on him as being famous now that he's not in the Ants any more. I just think he's really good looking. I'd like to be a friend of his. Well, I'd like to go out with him, that's my ambition. But then there's somebody else, isn't there? I know deep down I'll never get anywhere with him. I just wish it wasn't true. I'm going out with someone now, but I still keep in contact with Chris. And if I go off him, I won't forget him: I've still got my scrapbooks and everything.

And so have I. Four volumes of carefully pasted cuttings and pictures. It is this retentiveness that makes teenage girls such a lucrative market. And how exploitable is this urge to collect not only the records, but the posters, tour programmes, fan club specials, books, magazines, and any other product companies wish to foist on them! Birthdays, names, measurements, likes and dislikes are all learned by heart, and fans can often relate more statistical information about an artist than he could himself, off-hand. Yet the picture they build up is the one they want to believe, with faults rationalized or glossed over, and virtues often invented. It is easy to create an idealized fantasy man with none of the flaws of real men, and to transfer those attributes on to an inaccessible, but real, star. For most, it's just a way of brightening up dull, ordinary lives: the cynical comments written in my scrapbooks show that even at my most infatuated, I knew half of what was written was lies. For a minority, though, the dream can become an obsession. It happens gradually, as Carol Bedford explained:

You realize that you could ask for an autograph, and then you start to think, 'Wouldn't it be nice if he knew my name?' I've tried to understand why that is important. Perhaps it's an inferiority complex... you got special status for length of service. When he singled you out, all those hours of waiting didn't seem to exist.

Carol's waiting ended after a record company Christmas party in 1971, when George Harrison asked her to stop wasting her life in such a way:

It was a very moving conversation because it showed he cared. It was also a low point because I realized I would have to quit. If that was the only thing I could give to him, then I would. It took two months to build up courage to even ask myself if I could survive without seeing him: could I go through a week without the most important thing in the world to me – watching George Harrison walk out of the building?

Carol had come to England from Dallas to follow her band. 'Polythene' Pat Dawson, on the other hand, was a fan in Liverpool before the Beatles became famous. She recounted her memories to Mike Evans in *Let it Rock* (July 1975):

There was a hierarchy of people who'd been watching them for a long time, and they were quite matey with us – they used to pull birds from this group. But when the newer fans arrived, they were already beginning to get 'distanced'. The older fans tended to like them for their music, and as fellas in the personal sense, whereas the newer ones liked them because they were the Beatles. This was long before they made records or anything, but they were already a big cult in Liverpool. It wasn't like seeing people who were stars. You still saw them as a bunch of lads you might get off with.

As they became better known, many of the early fans refused to buy the records, not wanting their boys to leave them. Pat clearly recalls her sadness at their success:

The night Bob Wooler [the Cavern DJ] announced as they were going on stage that 'Please Please Me' had reached number one, it was awful, because the reaction was the opposite to what they expected. Everyone was stunned. That was the end of it as far as we were concerned.

Men became obsessed, too, of course. But the difference between, say, the man who changes his name to Elvis and the woman who spends all her savings following Spandau Ballet to the USA is that, for her, a close, socially acceptable relationship – marriage – is at least a possibility, no matter how remote. It is also difficult for a woman to actually fantasize about *being* her hero in the same way as a man could. With so few role models to follow, to fantasize about being on stage as a *female* performer may be almost a contradiction in terms. Instead, most of us dream of being a pop star's girlfriend: fame and recognition by proxy. Girls are taught to wait for men to give us what we want, rather than to get it ourselves. In the world of the Mills and Boon romance, passion, wealth, status and excitement are conferred on the passive heroine by the men who come into her life. That idea is a persistent one. My favourite daydream in boring classes at school was of a famous star suddenly walking into the room to take me away, leaving my classmates sighing in regret that they hadn't realized I was so wonderful. I felt that my lover could actually transform me, and many of my friends have confessed to similar Cinderella fantasies.

While women are judged – and taught to value

themselves – by the status of their men, they will continue to follow personable young groups. Perhaps, even, the most obsessive are also the most ambitious. Most of the fans I have met waiting outside studios and concert halls have been bright, energetic, articulate young women – hardly the stereotypical 'groupie' described in the songs, videos and fantasies of the Real Men of rock'n'roll.

The term 'groupie' is a dangerous one, for it is often used as a putdown for *any* woman involved in the industry. In February 1969, the newly formed *Rolling Stone* magazine devoted a whole issue to 'Groupies: The Girls of Rock', explaining to the reader that 'Some of the girls of rock, girls who are very much part of the scene – everybody knows them – never were groupies in the strict sense, but are somehow cut from the same fabric. Like Trixie, the girl bass-player, and Dusty, the girl recording engineer.' Pauline Black told of similar false assumptions being made by men when she was the singer in the Selecter, on the 2-Tone national tour:

Guys, when they're on the road, have a different attitude to when they're at home, and invariably I'd find myself with a whole load of young girls outside my door saying, 'Oh, so-and-so's thrown me out of his room because I won't do whatever.' Really young, naive girls who were just into the whole thing and had come back to the hotel expecting to have a bit of a drink and a good time without thinking of the consequences of hanging around hotels with loads of guys.

If a woman wishes to be involved in any way, it is often assumed that she is only there, ultimately, because she is attracted to the men. It is worth bearing this in mind whenever the term 'groupie' is used. And then there's the question of how 'groupies' see themselves. Pat Hartley, an American woman involved in the New York-Andy Warhol–music scene, when interviewed by *Spare Rib* (1974), saw it as a form of autonomous female activity:

The whole groupie thing turned itself around. It used to be that the guys could pick and choose. Well, after the first three years it was us choosing, the guys had no choice. In the end, when the groups came to town, the girls would decide whether . . . I mean, after having Stevie Winwood, was it worth it to have anyone less? And for the groups, in a way it was part and parcel of selling the albums. It was 1964 that the Beatles first came to the States, and around that year the groupies started. It was a different kind of thing then: the place was littered with 14-year-old girls, and there were people like me, Jenny Dean, Devon and others who were going into it from an intelligent point of view. We'd just find out who was in town and what hotel they were in. It's not that difficult, if one decided to put a little effort behind it. It's a society of a kind, the way it functions, it has its own strange rules. A lot of it is women dressing for women; a lot of it had to do with the competition between the chicks. We paired off in twos and there were always couples who were like married couples. Very few chicks would go in one at a time. Going in twos was sort of an adventure and it was fun. It was a weird thing. When it started, it started like a teenage sex vibe . . . all those women standing outside the Plaza Hotel screaming our knickers down for these incredible pop groups, and at the time, it really was the girls after the boys.

The freedom to be used by the consumer of your choice. But what happens when the stars themselves are women? Girls scream at girls, too. When the Ronnettes or the Shangri-Las played to a live audience, the front rows were full of young women screaming, reaching and hand-dancing in their seats. The girl group era told women that they could be stars, that they could dress up and look strong and sexy, get up there with the boys. 'I knew I was going to sing,' says Ronnie Spector firmly on the video of Alan Betrock's book *Girl Groups*. 'I knew, I had no qualms, nothing. I was going to sing, and I was going to sing rock'n'roll.' For Ronnie it was 13-year-old Frankie Lymon, a boy with a girl's high voice, who showed the way. For the girls watching her, Ronnie herself was opening up new possibilities. The girl groups told young women that their dreams were possible, and even as their songs reinforced the most reactionary ideas of love and marriage ('He Hit Me, And It Felt Like A Kiss'), they were showing that it *was* possible to be something more than somebody's girlfriend: a singer and a star.

In the August 1982 issue of *Ms* magazine, Marcia Gillespie talks of the significance for black girls of one of the few groups to survive the Beatles and the British invasion that followed:

> The Supremes were important – symbols of the idea that integration could happen, that we could make it and still have the dream. That black girls could be glamorous and beautiful and celebrated for it – at home and abroad ... The idea that black managers and recording companies could take three girls from the ghetto, take rhythm and blues, and move it and them from the back of the bus and to a limousine was daring and visionary for its time.

Women have continued to idolize women, to pin them up and objectify them in just the way any boy would. In the late 1970s, the most popular pin-up in girls' bedrooms was not John Travolta or Johnny Rotten, but Debbie Harry. It's often hard to tell if they just want to *be* them, or if they are in love with them. In adolescence, the line is thin between admiration and lust (*boys* screamed at both Bolan and Bowie) – although, with a little help, most of us grow out of it and become as anti-gay as the society which raised us. Helen Terry describes her relationship with her Culture Club fans:

> I get loads of letters, and the other day I met two girls with 'I love Helen Terry' scratched on their arm. That's really beyond me – all these girls screaming, 'I really love you!' It's so unreal. I think half of it is that they'd like to *be* me, they'd like to be close to George, to be able to sing, maybe. The other half is that, basically, I'm very safe: I'm like everyone's best mate, I talk to anyone. I'm fairly low-key.

On the whole, the word 'fans', when applied to women, is derogatory. It is always assumed that they are attracted to a person for the 'wrong' reasons, that they are uncritical and stupid. As an audience, they are usually treated with contempt by both bands and record companies. The 'real' audience is assumed to be male, and advertisements, record sleeves, and even stage presentation, are nearly always aimed at men. Yet a substantial majority of women own a tape- or record-player, and music is a constant background to our lives – on the radio at home, piped into supermarkets and factories, in the disco, records played while we do our chores. And in the brief time when the majority of girls *are* actively involved as fans, the fun and the thrills are unlike anything most men will ever experience. For us, in 1975, the real excitement had little to do with the Bay City rollers: it was about ourselves.

This is Olive, 1983. Siouxsie Sioux, former waitress from Chiselhurst, was the woman whose looks most influenced the class of '77. (photo: Kerstin Rodgers)

The Slits. (photo: Dennis Morris)

CHAPTER EIGHT

NKERAMA

SUE STEWARD

The soft-focus nostalgia of so many retrospective reports of the punk era often give the impression that women began producing – and consuming – pop music *circa* 1976. Before that, it sometimes seems, all they did was sing drooly pop songs forced on them by a fiendish manager . . . a character who supervised them from the wings, and ran off with more than his share of the money after the show ended. As audience members and record listeners they were, supposedly, most interested in soppy lyrics, and the heart-throb man singing them. They danced a bit, but mostly used pop as an outlet for sexual and, particularly, romantic fantasies. As soon as real-life romance came along, their interest in pop music waned altogether. *Real* pop, especially rock'n'roll, was for the boys. Mentions of female instrumentalists were sparse and frequently patronizing and belittling. So what did happen in 1976?

Punk played a vitally important role in women's new visibility. Initially, the music press and record companies were stand-offish and derisory, leaving the fanzines and independent record companies to report, comment on and produce the new music. Caroline Coon, Jonh Ingham and Vivien Goldman from *Sounds* were all exceptions to this and all were to define punk in the terms later taken up by fanzines. But, by and large, punk wanted to move faster than the conventional media.

For a while, there was quite a female mafia encircling the Sex Pistols coterie. It was they who often seemed to run the show: in Soho pubs, they plotted; in the streets and clubs, they laid plans for extracting vast sums of money from tyrant record companies. Schemes abounded for themselves and their bands. Malcolm McLaren got all the credit for punk and the Pistols, becoming the public face. However, at home and in their jointly owned shop Sex (later Seditionaries), McLaren relied on the sanity, clarity and dedication of his lover/partner, Vivienne Westwood, to realize their joint-projects. And in the offices of Glitterbest, the company which backed the Sex Pistols, Sophie Richmond was indispensable. For three years, she literally organized the Sex Pistols' lives, timetabled their days, bought their flats, paid their bills, and baled them out of trouble: the typical surrogate parent whom pop stars come to expect and demand.

After the bubble burst, Sophie turned to editing fiction, which she'd always preferred to pop music, anyway. Vivienne Westwood moved from dressing the Sex Pistols and their clones to Malcolm's subsequent protégés – BowWowWow – later converting her underground success into an international reputation as a fashion designer.

Managing Adam Ant was Jordan, who'd started out selling clothes in Seditionaries. For many years, she was a background figure, a 'conceptualist' and make-up artist for him. She even tried performing – disastrously – herself, and after setting her personal seal on the era with a magnificently statuesque role in Derek Jarman's punk epitaph, *Jubilee*, retreated to rural life to manage her husband's band.

Then there was Vermillion, a new breed on the music-business scene: a strident and vivid American woman whose 'won't take no shit' attitude was shocking in London music even then. She has remained in the trade, working as a PR for small rock'n'roll reissue labels, her fieriness still intact.

Barbara Harwood organized rehearsals, humped equipment, and drove the van for the Slits – who all seemed so petulant, demanding and spoilt. Barbara was like a kind of eccentric, leather-clad, elder sister, her own two kids always in tow.

Barbara Gogan was one of the few female musicians in this immediate circle around the Glitterbest empire. She was frustrated, treading water, and dreaming of a group (it became the

Jordan's lightning-striped make-up remains an emblem
of the time.   (photo: Shirley O'Loughlin)

Passions). She envisaged putting her theories of
independent music-making into practice – *and*
playing her guitar and singing, which she hadn't
done since the demise of the Derelicts, one of the
only bands featuring women on the pub rock-
benefit circuit. The Passions brought her chart
success with 'I'm in Love with a German Film
Star'. After they split, she moved to New York to
train as an actress.

These women – and journalists like Jane Suck,
Chrissie Hynde, Caroline Coon, and Vivien
Goldman – were planning, day and night. On the
sidelines, Judy Vermorel was taking notes which
she later combined with Sophie Richmond's
diaries to produce *The Sex Pistols*. In leather and
mohair, boots and jeans, they cut a sharp and
threatening image on the streets of Soho, where
they looked invincible and fearless.

FLASHPOINT

Punk has been unanimously acclaimed as the
starting-, breaking- and flashpoint of the last
decade's pop music. The frantic, loud, 4/4 time of
a thousand punk songs celebrated inability and
anti-virtuosity: the equivalent, in musical terms,
of what Vivienne Westwood called 'confrontation
dressing'.

Punk did have its shortcomings. It was a short-
lived era: two years at the most. It was urban,
concentrated mostly in London, Birmingham,
Leeds, Manchester, Liverpool and Glasgow. And,
from the start, it was white – apart from Poly
Styrene. For the majority of black and Asian
women, it had little or no relevance. Nevertheless,
it was a movement that thoroughly disrupted
the yawning chasm between performer and
audience, previously taken for granted. It was

accordingly easier than ever before for girls to get up there with the boys – and to do so without dragging their stereotypical images with them. After all, there's not much difference between the noise made by girls who can't play their instruments, and boys. In the words of bass-player Marion Fudger, then with the Art Attacks:

> That's when women started appearing because the emphasis wasn't on technical expertise – and women came in playing all kinds of things because of the extra confidence from knowing they didn't have to be brilliant. The whole expression was about anarchy – to do and say whatever you felt like at the time. It was great!

In black leather jacket and torn jeans, deathly pale and sullenly staring from dark-ringed eyes, Gaye Advert presented a mean and moody metaphor of punk's nihilism. She was a bass-player. She was a girl. But mostly she was 'Pretty Vacant'. Debates about whether or not she could play were mere gestures, as Gaye's group, the Adverts, acknowledged in their hit single, 'One Chord Wonders' (1977):

> *I wonder how he'll answer when you say*
> *We don't like you, go away.*
> *Come back when you've learnt to play . . .*

Punk was also a reaction to the rigid polarization in popular music into two distinct categories: pop and rock (black American dance-floor music – disco – and Jamaican reggae being virtually ignored by the UK media). Rock's roots lay in the progressive 1960s and was quasi-art music for 'serious' fans – a world of albums and in-depth interviews. Its stars, as often as not, emerged rarely from the stockbroker belt to muse. They were men with screaming axes and screeching genitals. Pop, in contrast, came directly from the familiar world of Tin Pan Alley, which produced

an endless string of disposable singles, and was dismissed as mere fodder for the teenybop market – comprised mainly of young girls. Punk rejected rock's hippy naturalism and pop's artless synthetics: peace and love, idealism and teenage romance were out; hate, war, negativity and sexual vulgarity were in. Reggae, a music born of struggle and disaffection, was adopted as an expression of punk's own sense of alienation.

THE DIY DEPARTMENT

Since the early 1970s, the major record companies had been limiting their artists to megastars, and were oblivious to the new music and the new bands. But punk changed all that. In obscure little pubs and clubs on both sides of the Atlantic, boys and girls were taking to the stage and dance-floor, to extol the peculiarities of the late 1970s social decay in screams, stares, and safety-pins. In small demo studios and on 4-track machines, in back-bedrooms and garages, groups were DIY-ing their own records and, in the UK, selling themselves through Rough Trade, the collective that was addressing the issues of independence rather than piracy. Working within a more recognizably political framework, Rough Trade's plan was to initiate new ways of producing and releasing music, making it available to young audiences *and* musicians who would otherwise not have had access to the emerging underworld.

The new style came of age in Jubilee Year (1977) with the Sex Pistols' 'God Save the Queen' topping the charts. The sacrilegious assaults went beyond the monarchy and the multi-nationals to become a culture-wide iconoclasm. In the face of the recession, the punks kidded themselves that they made a complete break with all that had gone before: a product of the present, with no past and no future.

Gradually during the 1970s, black conscious-ness through Rastafarianism had been working up a cohesive lifestyle. As 1976 headlines like 'Black Youth Run Riot at [Notting Hill] Carnival' proved, Rasta posed a threat to a society ever anxious to assimilate. American soul and r'n'b had fired the imagination of the mods, and ska and bluebeat had identified 1960s Rude Boys. Now, in the mid-1970s, narcissistic punks staged their indulgent style-wars, orchestrated street clashes in the Kings Road, to a soundtrack of punk songs and imported Jamaican reggae.

During a period of increasing unemployment and disaffection, the problems of race and class were more pointed than ever. In January 1978, two middle-class schoolgirls from Kingston, Jamaica, were occupying the number one position in the UK charts, with a single that had been

Toyah Willcox, as the chubby, violent punk in the film 'Jubilee'. She metamorphosed via a bewildering assortment of mythological characters – always heroic and glamorous, and drawn from her own imagination. (photo: courtesy of Cinegate Film Distribution Ltd.)

bought by thousands of punks while still on import. With its UK release, the infectious rhythms and chanted patois received maximum airplay, putting Althea and Donna's 'Uptown Top Ranking' into the national spotlight. And yet, when Donna and Althea appeared on *Top of the Pops* in sloppy T-shirts and khaki shorts, they certainly didn't present the gilt-edged glamour that seemed to accompany most black female singers at the time . . . Like punk itself, contemporary black music was challenging dominant social expectations. Despite other differences, common to both punk and reggae is their self-conscious appraisals of their positions within society.

GIRLS, GIRLS, GIRLS: WOMEN IN ROCK
In the 1970s, women exploded on to the rock stage in 'leather and studs, wielding electric guitars'. Not only did they occupy areas of music-making previously closed to them, but women also broke out of the shrine in which old rock myths had enclosed them. Instrumental in their change of (self-) image was the growth, impact and diffusion of feminism and the women's movement.

Suddenly, from out of the blue, there were a lot more women around, working in *all* the processes of record production. Much of the writing about these new arrivals, though, left out what was specifically different about them: their music, the sources they drew on, how they saw themselves, what they hoped for or thought they could achieve, what messages they thought they were passing on to their audiences – particularly to any girls who might be inspired by them to recognize new potentials for themselves. After all, these were among the questions being put to the 'new wave' of young men at the same time.

Part of punk's significance for women and girls rested on its rejection of what might be called the conventions of traditional sexuality. Both

The Mo-Dettes gained a reputation for their intense antipathy towards feminism and the women's movement.
(photo: David Corio)

the hippy idea of free 'permissive' love *and* the straighter conventions of love, romance and engagement rings were attacked, undermined and repudiated outright. In every way, punk sexuality was angry and aggressive, implicitly feminist. But once punk and gender started to be talked and written about – often by feminist-influenced women and girls – the same old thing happened: *all* women's and *all* girl's performances were lumped together into one single category, 'Women in Rock'. As an example, 'Women and Popular Music, 1976–81' (*Spare Rib*, 1981) collapsed together performers as diverse as Bessie Smith, Dusty Springfield, Aretha Franklin, Patti Smith, Poly Styrene and the Nolans. Certainly, they have a common gender. But between Dusty Springfield and Patti Smith, Poly Styrene and the Nolans there lies at least 15 years of social shifts and technological developments. Three thousand

miles separate Patti Smith from Poly Styrene. Poly and the Nolans took diverging routes to specific markets. Which is not even to consider that most fundamental difference of all – how they express and view their common position as women and entertainers.

AFTER-EFFECTS

The notion of 'independence' today is a spurious yardstick of women's relative involvements with men – economically, emotionally, or creatively. Now, the label 'independent woman' encompasses everything from the *Cosmo*-supergirl's overriding ambition for financial and career independence from men, to autonomous separatists who eschew any relationships with men whatsoever. But on all points of the spectrum, women are at least aware of, and mostly affected by, the ideas of feminism.

Things have changed since the mid-1970s when the key motivations for the punk women were optimism, iconoclasm, and an unflinching determination to get what *they* wanted. White pop music has again become seriously compartmentalized. Arri Upp (the Slits) called her generation 'The New Age Steppers'; their unity initially lay in their united struggle against the lifestyles, tastes, and philosophies of the previous decade. Without any fuss, the girls were as much a part of the vanguard as the boys – which in itself separated their generation from all that went before.

The rush of success, the sense of ground gained, and the arrogance this brought, created a sharply critical, unswervingly righteous generation of women. Though the majority of them never sheltered under the umbrella of feminism, they shared many of its ambitions and analyses.

Since then, as is always the case in pop music, the changes have been fast. Punk enthusiasm and principled disregard for material gains gave way to straightforward money deals, vast advances, and the big labels walked off with the bands. There has been no shortage of volunteers willing to play by the rules again. Many of those who had intentionally placed themselves on the margins made a reassessment: punk's puritanism was tailing into poverty and acrimony – and it no longer seemed politically desirable or essential to aim solely for the independent charts. A new 'radical' entrepreneurial outlook guided the growth of outfits like the Human League and the production/management group British Electric Foundation (BEF), and their performing profit centre, Heaven 17. The idea was to be popular, to make money, and to do some subversion from within, through marketing, video images and pseudo-political lyrics.

In this new era, women continue to play a part, and are not willing to return to the role the 1960s allocated them. In the wake of punk and particularly feminism's explosive effects on all areas of women's lives, there is no chance that they will relinquish all their gains. In the mid-1980s, women are back as singers, a glamorous focus for a group: Sade, Carmel, Helen Terry, Annie Lennox and Vi Subversa are central to their bands. But it is no longer enough to be 'just a singer': Annie Lennox also plays flute and keyboards, Vi Subversa is the Poison Girls' guitarist, and Alannah Currie is percussionist with the Thompson Twins. Women instrumentalists are making their presence felt in the success-story of mixed bands: Sarah Lee in the departed Gang of Four, Gillian Gilbert in New Order, and the increasing presence of black women musicians – not just singers – in bands like Abacush and African Woman.

Women-only gigs and bands – a strategy dating from the 1970s – are now familiar features of the landscape: both musicians and audience can find themselves at mixed and separatist events on consecutive nights of the week. Workshops are the age-old way of spreading skills at grassroots level. From the cocooned and supportive atmosphere of all-girls or all-women classes, a proliferation of workshops in most major towns guarantees a continuing flowering of confident and skilful players in pop.

It is 20 years since Sandie Shaw was the new face of the year, and Tina Turner was danced to across the country as she sang 'River Deep Mountain High'. As the decor, design and clothes buffs return to the 1960s for ideas, the revival of the careers of both these two women – Sandie via the distinctly post-feminist songs and music of the Smiths, and Tina through a revival of a Beatles song and a BEF production – point to the unpredictability and the continuity of popular music, and women's place in it.

Danielle Dax: the face of post-punk *femme fatale*. (photo: Kerstin Rodgers)

DISPENSING WORDS

RELEVANT READS

Girl Groups: The Story of a Sound by Alan Betrock, London: Omnibus Books 1982.

Sirens of Song: The Popular Female Vocalist in America, by Aida Pavletich, New York: da Capo 1980.

New Women in Rock by various authors, London: Omnibus Books 1982.

Superwomen of Rock by Susan Katz, New York: Tempo Books 1978.

Rock'n'Roll Women by Katherine Orloff, Los Angeles: Nash 1974.

'Rockabilly Women' by Robert K. Oermann and Mary A. Bufwack, from *Journal of Country Music*, vol. 8, no. 1, Nashville, 1979.

Rockabilly Queens: The Careers of Wanda Jackson, Janis Martin, Brenda Lee, etc. by Bob Garbutt, Ducktail Press, 1979.

Songs of Self-assertion: Women in Country Music by Mary A. Bufwack and Robert K. Oermann, New England Press.

American Women in Jazz, 1900 to the present: Their Words Lives and Music by Sally Placksin, New York: Wideview Books 1982.

Singers and Sweethearts: The Women of Country Music by Joan Dew, New York: Doubleday 1977. Loretta Lynn, Tammy Wynette, June Carter, Dolly Parton, Tanya Tucker.

Ma Rainey and the Classic Blues Singers by Derrick Stewart-Baxter, London: Studio Vista 1970. Mamie Smith, Rosa Henderson, Ma Rainey, Bessie Smith, Ida Cox, Victoria Spivey, Sippie Wallace, Alberta Hunter, etc.

The Boy Looked at Johnny by Julie Burchill and Tony Parsons, London: Pluto Press 1978. See the chapter called 'Girls'.

Any old way you choose it – 'Look at that stupid girl' on women, rock, sexism by Robert Christgau, London: Penguin 1973.

The Rolling Stone Reader: Janis Joplin, Joan Baez, Straight Arrow Books 1974.

The Guitar-Player Book: Interviews with Mary Osborne, Carol Kaye, Bonnie Raitt, New York: Grove Press 1978.

Boogie Lightning, New York: da Capo 1974. See chapters on the Chiffons and Aretha Franklin, by Michael Lydon and Ellen Mandel.

Sweet Saturday Night: Pop Song 1840–1920 by Colin McInnes, New York: Pantheon Arts 1967.

Motown and the Arrival of Black Music by David Morse, London: Studio Vista 1971.

Sound Effects by Simon Frith, London: Constable 1982. See the chapter called 'Rock and Sexuality.'

ML 3790 F74

'Popular music' – from *Is this your life?* analysis of rock lyrics by Terri Goddard, J. Pollock, Marion Fudger: London: Virago, 1977

The Electric Muse: The Story of Folk into Rock by Dave Laing, Karl Dallas, Robin Denselow, Robert Shelton, London: Methuen 1975.

The Soul Book by Ian Hoare, Clive Anderson, Simon Frith, Tony Cummings, London: Methuen, 1975.

Cool Cats: 25 Years of Rock'n'Roll Style London: Omnibus Press 1982. See 'Girls' style – worn-out career chic', by Cynthia Rose.

Stars by Richard Dyer, London: BFI 1979.

The Sex Pistols: The Inside Story by Fred and Judy Vermorel (with Sophie Richmond's diaries), London: Universal 1978.

As Serious as Your Life: The Story of the New Jazz by Val Wilmer, London: Quartet Books 1977. See chapter 11, 'It Takes Two People to Confirm the Truth', and chapter 12, 'You Sound Good for a Woman'.

Groupies and other Girls by John Burks and Jerry Hopkins, New York: Bantam 1970.

Groupie by Jenny Fabian and Johnny Byrne, London: Mayflower 1970.

Chase the Fade: Music, Memories, and Memorabilia by Anne Nightingale, London: Blandford Press 1981.

Encyclopedia of Rock, ed. Phil Hardy and Dave Laing, London: Aquarius 1977. Covers 1955–75 – excellent reference, more than rock.

BIOGRAPHIES

Daybreak: An Intimate Journal by Joan Baez, New York: Pantheon 1971.

Billie's Blues: The True Story of the Immortal Billie Holiday by John Chilton, London: Quartet 1975.

Bessie, Empress of the Blues by Chris Albertson, London: Abacus 1975.

Blondie, biography of Debbie Harry by Lester Bangs, London: Omnibus 1980.

Patsy Cline by Ellis Nassour, Tower 1981.

Meet on the Ledge: A History of Fairport Convention by Patrick Humphries, London: Eel Pie 1982.

Lady Sings the Blues by Billie Holiday and Willi022 Dufty: Penguin 1984.

Janis: Her Life and Times by Deborah Landau, New York: Warner 1971.

Coal Miner's Daughter by Loretta Lynn with George Vesey, Granada 1979.

A View from a Broad by Bette Midler, New York: Simon & Schuster 1980.

Joni Mitchell by Leonore Fleischer, New York: Flash Books 1976.

Midnight Baby, autobiography by Dory Previn, Elm Tree Books 1977.

Suzi Quatro by Margaret Mander, London: Futura 1976.

Diana Ross: An Illustrated Biography, by Geoff Brown, London: Sidgwick & Jackson 1981.

His Eye Is on the Sparrow by Ethel Waters with Charlie Samuels, Jove Pubs Inc. 1950.

Stand By Your Man by Tammy Wynette with Joan Dew.

MAGAZINES

'Women and Music', *Heresies*, issue no. 10 1980.

'Women, Music and Feminism', by Lindsay Cooper, in *Musics*, October 1977.

'Women in Music', Elizabeth Wood, *Signs*, vol. 6 no. 2.

'Women in Rock' – including interviews with Carol Kaye, June Millington (Fanny), Charlotte Caffey (Go-Go's), by Jas Obrecht *Guitar Player*, March, 1983.

Let it Rock, women's issue July 1975.

'Hooked on Love: Romance, and Sex and Song Lyrics', Simon Frith *New Society*, July 1981.

'The Voices of Women', Simon Frith, *New Society*, November 1981.

'Explained Melody: Interview with Joni Mitchell', Leyla Farrah, *International Musician and Record World*, July 1983.

'Rock and Sexuality', Simon Frith and Angela McRobbie, *Screen Education*, no. 29 1978–9. See also the reply 'Disco-Pleasure-Discourse: On "Rock and Sexuality" ', Dave Laing and Jenny Taylor, *Screen Education*, no. 30 1979.

'Typical Girls', Karen Benson, ZG

'A Fist of Charm: Interview with Lucy Toothpaste',

Juliet Ash, ZG.

'Sisterhood Is Powerful: American Women's Music Industry', Michele Kort, *Mother Jones*, July 1982.

'Collusion'

No. 1: 'Wild Women with Steak Knives: Diamanda Galas', Hannah Charlton; 'Silence Is a Rhythm, too', Vivien Goldman.

No. 2: 'Ghosts in the Hit Mythology: Interview with Carol Kaye', Sue Steward; 'Northern Soul: Gracie Fields', Simon Frith.

No. 3: 'Airtime: Two Women DJs, Sheila Tracy and Ghita Bala', Sue Steward; 'Androgynous Heart-throbs: Confessions of a Bay City Rollers Fan', Sheryl Garratt; 'Boys in Rock', Caroline Scott.

No. 4 'Queens of the Keyboard: Florence de Jongh and Ena Barga – Silent Movie Accompanists', Kate Ogburn; ESG: The Family Jewels', Steven Harvey; 'The Image of Women in Haitian Music', Gloria LeGros.

No. 5: 'Lord, If You're a Woman: Interview with Darlene Love (ex-Chiffons)', Mick Patrick; There'll Always be Stars in the Sky: Interview with Lata Mangeshkar'; 'One from the Heart: Interview with Connie Francis', Mary Harron.

'Spare Rib'

No. 5: 'Dana Gillespie: Interview', Marion Fudger.

No. 6: 'Women in Music: Gail Colson (label manager, Charisma), Helen Walters (press officer, RSO), Lisa Denton (head of press, Phonogram)'; 'Honky Tonk Women', Carmel Knerber talks to Fanny.

No. 11: 'Roll Over and Rock Me Baby', Margaret Geddes on fans and groupies.

No. 14: Pat Hartley talking to Marion Fudger about groups and being a groupie.

No. 18: 'Women in Music: Anne Nightingale interviewed', Marion Fudger.

No. 19: 'Women in Music: Conference with Maddy Prior, Marsha Hunt, Yvonne Elliman, Marion Fudger, Susie Watson-Taylor, with Rob Partridge', *Melody Maker* 1972.

No. 20: 'A Rap with Elkie', Elkie Brooks with Marion Fudger.

No. 21: 'Yeah, He Plays with Real Mammary: Interview with Ginni Whitaker (drums) and Dorothy Moscowitz (keyboards) from Country Joe and the Fish', Marion Fudger.

No. 22: 'Women in Music: Linda Lewis', Marion Fudger.

No. 23: 'I'm Not Going to Sing Nursery Rhymes: Joan Armatrading', Marion Fudger.

No. 24: 'Once More with Feeling: Why Aren't There More Women in Music', Marion Fudger.

No. 25: 'Women in Music: Anita Kerr (organist, pianist)', Marion Fudger.

No. 26: 'Women in Music: Terri Quaye', Marion Fudger.

No. 27: 'Mountain Women Blues', Sheila Rowbotham on *Traditional Songs by Working Women* (Rounder Records).

No. 28: 'Bridget St John: Interview', Marion Fudger.

No. 29: 'Women in Music: Goldie Zelkowitz (Goldie and the Gingerbreads, Genya Ravan)', Marion Fudger.

No. 30: 'The Only Thing is to "Do-It-Yourself" ', Saffron Summerfield on producing her first record; 'Interview with Ruth Bachelor (song-writer)' Marion Fudger.

No. 31: 'A Woman's Composing Is Like a Dog's Walking on his Hind Legs. It's Not Done Well, But You Are Surprised to Find It Done At All', Marion Lees on three female composers (Ethel Smyth, Alma Mahler, Clara Schumann).

No. 32: 'Dory Previn', Marion Slade.

No. 33: 'Frankie Armstrong: Interview', Marion Fudger.

No. 34: 'Women's Music from America', a checklist by Tony Russell.

No. 36: 'The Quota System and Black Shiny Handbags: Conference Report from Musicians' Union Debate about Women'.

No. 37: 'Images of Janis Joplin', Margaret Walters.

No. 38: 'I Love'em and Leave 'em', Liz Waugh and Terri Goddard on sexist lyrics.

No. 42: 'Peroxide Pol and the Counter Revolution: Tammy Wynette', Sue Tyrell.

No. 46: 'The Stepney Sisters Interview: Feminism and rock music – can they be combined?' Marion Fudger.

No. 48: 'Folk with Feeling: Interview with Peggy Seeger'.

No. 53: 'Stepping Out with Joan Armatrading: Interview', Marion Fudger.

No. 60: 'Women in Punk', Su Denim.

No. 72: 'Bessie Smith: The Gin-soaked Queen from Chattanooga', Alan Balfour.

No. 100: 'The Body Snatchers: Interview'.

No. 107: 'Women and Popular Music, 1976–81', Lucy Toothpaste.

No. 110: 'Rock around the Cock: Women and Sexuality', Lindsay Cooper.

Interesting finds in jumble sales and junk shops (back issues)

Let it Rock
Contradictions (Birmingham women's newspaper)
Jolt
Brass Lip
Shocking Pink
Drastic Measures
Cross Now
Spare Rib
Sing Out! (American folk)
Street Life
Woman Sound

DISPENSING WITH WORDS

RELEVANT RECORDS

This discography is arranged alphabetically, by artist.

African Woman, *African Women Abroad* (African Woman).
Althea and Donna, 'Uptown Top Ranking' (Front Line).
Les Amazones de Guinée, *Au Coeur de Paris* (Editions Enimas Conakry) (Guinea).
Amy and the Angels, 'Darling, Let's Have Another Baby' (Zick-Zack).
Laurie Anderson, *Big Science* (Warner Bros).
Joan Armatrading, *Joan Armatrading* (A&M).
Frankie Armstrong, Peggy Seeger and **Sandra Kerr**, *The Female Frolic* (Argo).
Art Bears, with **Lindsay Cooper, Georgie Born** and **Dagmar Krause**, *Hopes and Fears*, (Re Records).

Virginia Astley, *From Gardens Where We Feel Secure* (Rough Trade).
Asabia *Asabia* (Star Musique) (Ivory Coast).
Au Pairs, *Playing with a Different Sex* (Human).
LaVern Baker, *Real Gone Gal* (Charly reissue).
Beach Boys, with **Carol Kaye**, 'Good Vibrations' (Capitol).
Mbilia Bel, Mbilia Bel Avec Seigneur Ley Rocherau (Genidia) (Zaire).
Madeleine Bell, *Coming Atcha* (RCA).
Maggie Bell, *Queen of the Night* (Polydor).
Belle Stars, 'The Entertainer', produced by **Ann Dudley** (Stiff).
Louise Bennett, 'Yes M'Dear: Miss Lou Live* (Island).

163

Adele Bertei, 'Build Me A Bridge' (Geffen).
Janis Joplin, *Cheap Thrills* (Columbia).

B-52s, 'Hero Worship' (Island).
Blondie, with **Debbie Harry,** *Parallel Lines* (Chrysalis).
BowWowWow, with **Annabella Lu Win,** *See Jungle* (RCA)
Elkie Brooks, *Rich Man's Woman* (A&M).
Ruth Brown, *Rockin' with Ruth Brown* (Charly reissue).
Kate Bush, 'Wuthering Heights' (EMI).
Kim Carnes, 'Betty Davis Eyes' (EMI).
Betty Carter, *An Audience with Betty Carter* (Bet-Car).
Meg Christian and Chris Williamson, *Live at Carnegie Hall* (Olivia).
Randy Crawford, *Nightlines (WEA).*
Celia Cruz, *La Incomparable Celia Cruz* (Seeco).

Danielle Dax, 'Popsykle' (United Dairies).
Delta 5, *See the Whirl* (Charisma).
Sandy Denny, *Like an Old-fashioned Waltz* (Island).

Sheena Easton, 'Modern Girl' (EMI).
Eek-a-Mouse, 'Anarexol' (Greensleeves).
ESG, 'You're No Good' (Fac/99 Records).

Marianne Faithfull, *Broken English* (Island).
Fanny, *Charity Ball* (Reprise).
Frank Chickens, 'We Are Ninjas' (KAZ).
Aretha Franklin, *Aretha's Gold* (Atlantic).
Fun Boy Three, 'Our Lips are Sealed' (Chrysalis).

Diamanda Galas, 'Wild Women with Steak Knives' (Y).
Astrud Gilberto, *The Astrud Gilberto Album* (Verve).
Girls School, *Demolition* (Bronze).
Vivien Goldman with Sylvian Vanian, 'Chantage' (Celluloid).
Go-Gos, *Vacation (IRS).*
The Best of Shirley and Lee with **Shirley Goodman,** (Ace reissue).
Marcia Griffiths, *Steppin',* produced by **Sonia Pottinger** (Sky Note).

Nina Hagen, *Nina Hagen Band (CBS).*
Emmylou Harris, *The Best of Emmylou Harris* (Warner Bros).
The Hassans with **Nazia Hassan,** *Disco Deewane (EMI).*
Heart with **Nancy Wilson** and **Anne Wilson,** *Dreamboat Annie* (Mushroom).
Nona Hendryx, *Design for Living* (RCA).
Billie Holiday, *The Original Recordings* (CBS).

Millie Jackson, *Caught Up* (Polydor).
Etta James, *The Best of Etta James* (United Superior Records).
Jam Today, 'Stereotyping' (Stroppy Cow).
Jefferson Airplane with **Grace Slick,** *Surrealistic Pillow* (RCA).
Grace Jones, *Nightclubbing* (Island).
Lambert, Hendricks and Annie Ross, *Sing a Song of Basie* (Impulse/Jasmine).
Kid Creole and the Coconuts with **Carol Colman,** (bass) *Tropical Gangsters* (Island).
Carole King, *Tapestry* (Ode).
King Trigger with **Trudy Baptiste,** *River* (Chrysalis).
Eartha Kitt, *The Best of Eartha Kitt* (MCA).

Patti LaBelle and the Bluebelles, *Early Hits* (Trip).
Brenda Lee, *The Best of Brenda Lee* (Tee-Vee Records).
Laura Lee, 'Women's Love Rights' (Hot Wax).
The Lijadu Sisters, *Horizon Unlimited* (Afrodisia) (Nigeria).
Lora Logic, *Pedigree Charm* (Rough Trade).
Julie London, *Julie is her Name* (Edsel reissue).
M'pongo Love, *M'Pongo Love* (Safari Ambiance) (Zaire).
Lena Lovich, 'Lucky Number' (Stiff).
Lulu, *The Most of Lulu* (MFP).
Barbara Lynn, *Here is Barbara Lynn* (Oval).
Barbara Lynn and **Bettye Swan,** *Elegant Soul* (Atlantic).
Loretta Lynn, *The Loretta Lynn Story* (MCA).

Kirsty MacColl, 'There's a Guy Works Down the Chipshop Thinks he's Elvis' (Polydor).
The Mahatolla Queens, *Phezulu Eqhudeni* (Earthworks) (South Africa).
Malaria, *Revisited* (ROIR cassette).
Lata Mangeshkar, *Bengali Modern Songs* (EMI India).
Tania Maria, *Come with Me* (Picante).
Rita Marley, *Who Feels It Knows It* (Trident).
Bette Midler, *The Divine Miss M* (Atlantic).
The Mistakes, *Live at the Caribbean* (Mistakes Music).
Joni Mitchell, *Ladies of the Canyon* (Reprise).

Judy Mowatt, *Black Woman* (Island).
Maria Muldaur with **Kate** and **Anna McGarrigle,** **Linda Rondstadt** and **Bobbye Hall Porter,** *Waitress in a Donut Shop* (Reprise).

New Order with **Gillian Gilbert,** 'Blue Monday' (Factory).
Maggie Nichols and **Julie Tippetts,** *Sweet and S'Ours* (Free Music Productions).
Nico, *Chelsea Girls* (Reprise).

Hazel O'Connor, *Breaking Glass* (A&M).

Dolly Parton, 'Jolene' (RCA).
Annette Peacock, *X Dreams* (Aura).
Penetration with **Pauline Murray,** *Don't Dictate* (Virgin).
Poison Girls with **Vi Subversa**, *Hex* (Xntrix).
Flora Purim, *Stories to Tell* (Milestone).
Pulsillama, 'The Devil Lives in my Husband's Body' (Y).

Suzi Quatro, '48 Crash' (Bell).
Queen Ida, *Queen Ida in New Orleans* (Sonet).

The Raincoats, *Odyshape* (Rough Trade).
Bonnie Raitt, *Home Plate* (Warner Bros).
Ranking Ann, *A Slice of English Toast* (Ariwa).
Rhoda and the Special AKA, 'The Boiler' (2-Tone).
The Runaways, *Queens of Noise* (Mercury).

The Selecter with **Pauline Black**, *The Selecter* (2-Tone).
The Sequence, *Sugarhill Present the Sequence*, produced by **Sylvia Robinson** (Sugarhill).
Helen Shapiro, *Helen Hits Out/Tops with Me* (EMI double reissue).
Sandie Shaw, *The Sandie Shaw File* (Pye).
Nina Simone, *I Put a Spell on You*, (Phillips).
Siouxsie and the Banshees, *The Scream* (Polydor).
The Slits, *Cut* (Island).
Sly and the Family Stone with **Cynthia Robinson** and **Rose Stone**, *Family Affair* (Epic).
Bessie Smith, *The Empress* (CBS).
Patti Smith, *Horses* (Arista).
Valaida Snow, *HighHat Trumpet and Rhythm* (EMI).
Dusty Springfield, *The Best of Dusty Springfield* (Contour).
Yma Sumac, *Voice of the Xtaby* (EMI Regal).
Sweet Honey in the Rock, *Good News* (Flying Fish).

Carroll Thompson, *Hopelessly in Love* (C&B).
Richard and **Linda Thompson**, *I Want to See the Bright Lights Tonight* (Island).
Tom Tom Club with **Tina Weymouth**, *The Genius of Love* (Island).
Ike and **Tina Turner**, *Greatest Hits* (United Artists).
Two Sisters, *B-Boys Beware* (Streetwave).

Various, **Golden Ladies of Soul** (Pickwick).
Various, *Making Waves*, compilation featuring **Real Insects**, **Nancy Boys**, **Tango Twins**, **Sisterhood of Spit** and other all-women acts (Girlfriend).
Various, *Women of the Blues* (RCA).

Various, *Wonder Woman: The History of the Girl Group Sound*, vol. 1: 1961–4 (Rhino).
Various, *Southern Soul Belles* (Charly).
Velvet Underground with **Nico** and **Maureen Tucker**, *Velvet Underground with Nico* (Verve Select).

WARP-9, 'No Man Is an Island', produced by **Lotti Golden** and Richard Scher (Prism).
Waka Queen Salawa Abeni, *Ikilo* (Leader).
Dionne Warwicke, *Greatest Hits*, vols 1 and 2 (Warner Bros).
The Weather Girls, *Success* (CBS).
Weekend, 'A View from her Room' (Rough Trade).
Kitty Wells, *The Country Hall of Fame* (MCA Coral).
Tammy Wynette, *The Best of Tammy Wynette* (Epic).

X-Ray Spex with **Poly Styrene**, *Germ-free Adolescents* (EMI).
X-Ray Spex (**Poly Styrene**) and the Adverts (**Gaye**), *The Roxy, London WC2, January–April 1977* (EMI).

Yoko Ono, *Yoko Ono and the Plastic Ono Band* (Apple).

Every effort has been made to locate the copyright owners of the material quoted in the text. Omissions brought to our attention will be credited in subsequent printings. Grateful acknowledgement is made to the following publishers: Stiff Records for *One Chord Wonders* (The Adverts), CBS for *Success* (Weather Girls), Kaz Records for *Yellow Toast* (Frank Chickens), Sugarhill Records for *It's Good To Be the Queen* (Sylvia Robinson), Bell Records for *All of Us Love All of You* (Bay City Rollers).

INDEX